LAWNS, AND HOW TO MAKE THEM, TOGETHER WITH THE PROPER KEEPING OF PUTTING GREENS

LAWNS, AND HOW TO MAKE THEM, TOGETHER WITH THE PROPER KEEPING OF PUTTING GREENS

Leonard Barron

www.General-Books.net

Publication Data:

Title: Lawns, and How to Make Them, Together With the Proper Keeping of Putting Greens
Author: Barron, Leonard, 1868-1938
Publisher: New York : Doubleday, Page company
Subjects: Lawns

1

LAWNS, AND HOW TO MAKE THEM, TOGETHER WITH THE PROPER KEEPING OF PUTTING GREENS

PREFACE

THE main hope in this book is that it will result in more and better suburban gardens. I believe this volume is the first that has ever been written treating the making and maintenance of the ornamental lawn from a purely practical standpoint. Its purpose is to enable anyone to establish a respectable and adequate greensward in any sort of soil where grass can be made to grow.

The photographic illustrations, so graphic that they are essential to the story, have with few exceptions been made, expressly for the present purpose, by Herbert E. Angell, Henry Troth, Nathan R. Graves, and myself. Plates xix and xx are by courtesy of the U. S. Department of Agriculture.

Thanks for information in the matter of seeds and mixtures are especially accorded to W. E. Marshall and L. W. Wheeler; for cooperation in obtaining many of the pictures to John T. Withers, John Dunbar, and J. Featherstone. L. B.

New Tork, 1906.

The Perfect Lawn in an Ideal Setting (H. E. Angell) Frontispiece

FACING PAGE II. Radical Renovation (H. E. Angelt) 4 III. The First Steps in Lawn Making (H. E. Angelt). 5 IV. Making the Seed Bed (H. E. Angelt) 10

V. Cutting and Laying Sods (N. R.

LAWNS AND HOW TO MAKE THEM

A cruel answer to an everyday problem Remaking the best method-Fertilising Top dressing Mastering weeds and insects Futility of half-hearted methods Why English lawns are impossible The fallacy of the Newport lawns.

"WHAT can I do to my lawn to make it fresh and velvety again?" This, in some form or other, is the question that is asked by 90 per cent, of all who take an interest in their gardens and wish to keep the general appearance at par. It is the common question, too, that is asked by everyone as soon as he begins to take an interest in the grounds surrounding his home. As a matter of fact the question is usually more than justified. The lawn does need renovating.

"How to do it?" Well, the most effective result is attained by the most radical course. The best and simplest way to renovate the old lawn is to make a new one. Nine times out of ten it will not pay to patch, patch, and work interminably over a badly conditioned grass plot, simply because the necessary soil conditions for the good lawn are not there.

If the result that presents itself to the questioner is merely that of recent neglect that is to say a heretofore good lawn has been allowed to get out of control it may be recovered in one season without an undue expenditure of either labour or money. In such a case what is necessary is: firstly, a moderate cutting, preferably with the scythe and not going so closely to the roots that they will be unduly exposed to the drying influence of the sun; secondly, rolling and fertilising; and thirdly, watering and mowing and rolling for the rest of the season.

If, on a good soil, a lawn has become much overrun with weeds it can be brought under control again, and put into good condition, by scratching up the surface with a rake after removing the coarse weeds and seeding with one half the quantity of good recleaned grass seed that would be used for the making of a new lawn.

As a rule, however, it may be taken for granted that a lawn that really needs reno- If the natural best, break up tl art it off to fill a hollow spot, thus making room for a better soil THE FIRST STEPS IN LAWN MAKING vating, because it has gone so far to the bad as to present an appearance of anything in the world but a lawn, should be entirely remade. If the old lawn gave out because the grasses could not find any soil on which to grow, think you then that the new seed will do any better? Not a bit of it! You may add fertiliser, you may scatter bone-meal and wood-ashes in abundance, you may dress it with air-slaked lime in the fall, or you may top-dress abundantly, running the whole gamut of farm manures, but, believe me, you have a long fight ahead. It takes a great deal more than mere dressings of stable manure or chemical fertiliser to once again put the soil into "good heart."

The quick and sure method of doing this is by the plough. Or, if you only deal with a very small garden, do the work with a spade. It may mean the using up of a great deal of muscular force, but in the long run you will be the gainer. If it's in the fall, top-dress the soil, dig it over two spits deep, and leave it roughly heaped without any smoothing, whatever for the winter's frosts to act upon it. Frost is a wonderful agent in the mellowing of the soil and in the killing of obnoxious

Because of the extra-trying conditions of the American climate a much greater depth and more thorough preparation of soil are necessary. The price of a good lawn is eternal vigilance and persistent cultivation of the grass, so as to keep out the weeds.

Remember the precept of the Sunday school teacher: that the best way of keeping bad ideas and wicked thoughts from crowding into the mind is by occupying it thoroughly with good thoughts.

THE NEWPORT FALLACY

We are accustomed to hear much in praise of the lawns of Newport, but as a matter of fact they will not bear comparison for texture and quality of grasses with many that are found elsewhere. A very careful inspection of a great many of these famed swards has revealed to me that they owe their beautiful greenery just as much to the weeds that occupy the ground as they do to the grasses, and often indeed more so. What is accomplished is the fruit of diligent care, feeding and watering, for the land is not adapted to an ideal lawn. Unless you are on the same sort of sandy soil, and are willing to work incessantly, don't emulate a Newport lawn, but have something better that can be kept in good condition without a great deal of labour and expense.

CHAPTER II How TO MAKE A LAWN ONCE FOR ALL

Ground preparation Starting work ahead of the builders Uncomfortable newness The bugbear of inert soil Making new soil Barnyard manure and humus Lime Bad soil vs. bad seed Difficulty of reconstruction Clearing Ploughing Harrowing Corn or potatoes as a previous crop Cowpeas Final Enrichment Weeds.

MUCH is gained by deciding upon the site for the lawn and completing the preliminary steps for its preparation well in advance of the time that building operations are commenced. Indeed, the aim should be to lay out the lawn, roughly as to outline but complete as to the preparation of the soil, a year before the building contractors arrive. Unfortunately this is usually an impossible course, and though it may be followed out occasionally on large estates, where very often there is a great deal of general construction work to be carried out so as to fit it for human habitation, yet it is so rarely a practical possibility in connection with smaller plots as to be unworthy of consideration now.

Have a good supply of a rich uniform loam, evenly spread over the surface

Finally rake, or harrow, till the top soil is perfectly smooth and freed from all rubbish, such as roots, stones, etc. There is no better tool than a rake

MAKING THE SEED BED

CUTTING AND LAYING SODS

Turves are generally cut 12 inches wide, 2 inches thick, and a yard long. They can then be rolled for transport. After relaying, beat down very firmly. Turfing may be done in summer and the cutting of the sod will kill deeper-rooted weeds, thus giving a good grass lawn; but the process is very expensive

At the same time, even though one may not be able to make complete lawns before the house is built, it is very often perfectly practicable to make the larger lawn areas before the house is built a piece of foresight that will go far toward giving a comfortable setting and homelike atmosphere to the new dwelling. The appearance of newness is always disturbing, and so long as heavy construction work is being done around the home, there is a feeling of unrest that is disturbing to one's piece of mind.

Within the immediate vicinity of the building it is not so easy to preserve intact the lawn that was made before the building was begun. There are excavations for the foundation of the house and for the cellar space, the carting in of bricks, lumber, and other construction material, a majority of which will be dumped down or piled up very near to the place where building is going on so that they may be handled with the least expenditure of labour.

I have seen the lawn laid two years in advance and that too on a suburban lot. The ground space which was to be utilized by the builders was boarded over temporarily and although the grass was lost for a season, the labour of repairing was very little. The surface merely had to be lightly scarified, fine surface soil scattered over it, and grass seed distributed. By the middle of the season after this was done there was very little trace of there ever having been any damage at all.

Naturally when this course is followed all the refuse matter and debris from the building has to be carefully carted away and disposed of according to the most convenient method. This involves an amount of labour, however, that is not usually counted upon in making an estimate for the foundations and cellar of the house. '

Yet it would be a mighty good thing if it were always understood that the excavated earth be removed entirely or filled in at some point where it could be properly covered with fertile top soil in due course. Too often this inert, hard soil, which has never been brought under cultivation (and which in the ordinary course of events would take several years of close cultivation before it could be considered a good soil), is simply scattered around, generally as near the house as possible, burying completely whatever good soil was originally there. If there are unevennesses in the contour of the land, this excavated earth is used for the "fill and in after years the owner is consumed with wonderment as to why this or that particular spot in his garden is so unresponsive to cultivation.

If the excavated matter be evenly spread over the surface to a depth of only a few inches, and, after having received a good dressing of well rotted stable manure, the whole is turned under by thorough and careful trenching, the results will be satisfactory, for the buried top soil is thus once more brought to the surface. While this may be a satisfactory method it is not the course that is advised. Far better, indeed, is it to have the dug out soil entirely removed. For a good lawn you need, not a passably fertile soil, but the richest that the district will afford, and one that is in good tilth just such as you want for your vegetable garden.

MAKING A GOOD SOIL It is impossible to get soil too good for making a good lawn. A depth of one foot is absolutely necessary, but two feet is immeasurably better. If the ground be naturally good, and of fair depth of top soil, the site may be put into perfect lawn condition by deep ploughing without subsoiling.

If the ground be poor the preliminary steps in the making of the lawns must consist of heavily manuring or dressing with commercial fertiliser, the preference being with the former. On very light soils organic manure is vastly superior to the chemical fertiliser because it adds humus, with the result that it helps greatly to retain moisture, and, moreover, its actual food value is much more lasting. It may not yield such an abundance of readily available plant food at the start, but it will spread its benefits over a much greater time. Practically, barnyard manure is the best soil ameliorator; the chemical substances which are introduced for the purpose of supplying the equivalent food values do not achieve the same result in the same way.

Air-slacked lime might be spread on to the soil at the same time as the manure or after the first dressing of the latter has been turned under, using it at the rate of thirty or even forty bushels to the acre. This can be evenly spread over the surface and raked or harrowed until it is thoroughly incorporated with the upper layer of the soil. Lime assists clay soils by flocculating, and corrects the acidity of all soils.

Too much insistence cannot be placed upon this preliminary thorough preparation. Most lawn failures are due to neglect of this one fundamental thing. Not once in ten thousand times is a bad result due to bad or poor seed. It pays to buy well cleaned seed, however, such as is known as "fancy recleaned," rather than the light weight lower priced grades which though pure seed that is free from weeds contain also a very large percentage of chaff.

The very fact that the lawn is the foundation of the perfect garden is sufficient reason for insisting that it should be made in the best way we know. The expenditure of a few extra dollars per acre at this time will result in subsequent annual savings that will far outweigh the preliminary extra cost. There should be no misconception on this point. The lawn, more than any other part of the garden, must from the very nature of things be started properly, because it is a permanent crop, so to speak. Shrubberies can be re- planted; the flower borders can be entirely rearranged year by year, with but comparatively little trouble; the vegetable garden is generally cultivated, cropped, and fertilised twice a year; and, in each of these cases, it is an easy matter to add fertility whenever it becomes necessary.

But, with the lawn, it is far otherwise. Its reconstruction means the making over of such a vast area in comparison with the other parts of the garden, that though it may need it the work is likely to be deferred again and again, We see the result in hundreds of suburban gardens. The lawn surrounding the home utterly lacks that rich intense colour that seems to invite one within the confines of the garden, and the place is devoid of that reposeful air of comfort and luxury that the well nourished, well-kept lawn always imparts. The greensward is the one permanent feature of the home garden that is expected to be equally attractive from all points of view, at all times of the year, and in all succeeding seasons.

The ground which will eventually become the lawn must be cleared of all roots of trees and weeds removed, so far as possible. The ideal course to follow is this. First rough clear the ground. If the site is covered with trees or tree stumps which must be destroyed the tops can be cut down and the stumps and roots may be blown up with dynamite. A half pound charge will usually suffice for the removal of the average tree stump. The split and torn roots and stumps may be then grubbed out of the ground by hand labour and thrown into convenient piles. These may then be burned as they stand, and the ashes being distributed over the future lawn site, will be of material aid in improving the fertility of the soil.

After this, plough thoroughly, going as deeply as is reasonably convenient and turning the surface well under in doing so. Now harrow and cross harrow, using a sharp steel-toothed harrow which will also act as a drag to clear off any roots and other refuse that may not have been removed in the first place. In other words, prepare the site just as though you were starting in to turn it into good farm land; fertilising, ploughing, and harrowing, using the subsoil plough to break the hardpam if it is necessary to do so, to secure drainage on a heavy soil.

Now give it over to a crop of corn or potatoes and for one season before the actual lawn making begins treat it exactly as though it were farm land. The reason for this is that the regular cultivation given to either one of these crops will be of the greatest benefit in encouraging a good growth of the grass seed when it is sown the following fall or spring. Moreover, there will be a slight addition of humus, and any latent weed seeds will have germinated and the plantlets killed in the process of cultivation. On lands deficient in humus grow a crop of cowpeas and plough under in the fall; then give a dressing of lime.

The following season, or in the fall of the same year, another dressing of well rotted fertiliser, followed by ploughing and harrowing, will have brought the soil into proper condition. Land that will not grow a good crop of corn will never grow a good lawn. Attention to the growing crop of corn or potatoes assures cultivation of the land without the labour being a dead loss. After the crop is harvested spreah manure over the entire surface It is best to lay a narrow border of turf to make the margins of the future lawn, and scatter seed inside the area thus marked out

When sowing near the edge swing the forearm in a circular motion, letting the seed run from the bottom of the fist

MAKING TRUE EDGES of the ground at the rate of twenty tons to the acre, plough it under and harrow the entire surface very thoroughly, passing over every spot three or four times, travelling in different directions, and remove any stones or roots that may be brought to the surface. At this time, too, any unevenness of the contour must be remedied. If there is yet time allow the first crop of weeds to germinate, harrowing the surface when the plantlets are less than an inch high.

The Contour Rolling or level surface Preferred exposure No model grade Making the most of the offscape Scope for the artist The routine of the work Marking roads and paths Repairing the grade Levelling made easy Filling around trees Underdrainage and its purpose Importing top soil Dangers involved.

THE ideal lawn, except it be less than a quarter of an acre, is of a gently rolling contour, rather than a perfect level Nature does not, as a rule, lay down her surfaces in absolute levels. She does so in a bog or with water, but surely, we do not wish to create the impression that the spot selected for our country home has characteristics in common with these. We do not want the impression that the site is low lying and damp. The slightly rolling contour obviates this, and, further, it is pleasing to the eye in a variety of ways. It facilitates the future planting and enables the landscape picture to be more harmonious, better balanced.

The very small lawn, however, had perhaps better be a level one. There is not within its confines room for rolling contour in proportion to the surrounding masses of shrubs. And further a level spot sufficient for a tennis court is desirable in the majority of cases. If the ground itself slopes to such an extent that there is any great difference between the two ends of such a space, the result will be better by resorting to a terrace, and here let it be said that wherever possible the more pleasing effect will be attained by placing the house on the high part of the terrace.

One cannot always choose the exposure for the lawn. By preference it should be to the south and east rather than to the north and west, because of the greater warmth of those aspects and the consequent earlier appearance of verdure in the spring.

GETTING A GRADE In reality it is far easier to do the grading of the ground than it is to explain lucidly how to set about it. Since there are no absolute laws to be followed the whole matter of the grade being one of artistic appreciation it is only possible to explain the routine of the work and the general principles that should be adopted.

There can be no such thing as a model grade for any one place. There may be a model grade for a certain combination of circumstances, but as these are changeable factors, varying according to the fancy or taste of the individual, it cannot be said that any given grade is the right one for a given area at all times. There may be a variety of equally good contours which would fit in with the surroundings just in the same way as there are a variety of bad contours which cannot be harmonious.

As a general rule the grading should be in harmony with the general slope of the land and designed to hide, more or less, paths and driveways that would otherwise be too prominent. To take a concrete example, for instance, refer to the illustration, Plate xxxi The grading in this case has been very skilfully accomplished to obscure the driveway which runs completely arour. d the lawn and in front of the belt planting of rhododendrons and other shrubs. Though to all appearances a perfect level, the entire lawn is actually shaped like a shallow saucer that is, it is higher at the sides than it is in the centre. The consequence is that, standing at any given point, the driveway is not seen, unless the position of the observer is right on it. Even then there is only a few feet of drive seen in the very foreground. The belt planting fits in well with this particular contour.

Grading to a pleasing roll is a matter purely of artistic appreciation for which no paper rules can be made. It is here indeed that the landscape architect has the greatest chance for expressing his art. The best contours are never apparent. So sure as the rolls become obtrusive and prominent they are bad. An unbalanced contour will destroy the sense of proportion between the lawn and its surroundings and very often has the effect of making the house look like an excrescence on the landscape instead of nestling comfortably into it.

SEQUENCE OF OPERATIONS

After the ground has been smoothed over in the first rough treatment, is the time to establish the grades, after which the other construction work should be attacked in this order: 1. Ploughing, following the first plough with the subsoiler in the same furrow, if the subsoil is hardpan.

2. Harrowing, using a disc harrow to cut the clods and finishing with a fine toothed or smoothing harrow.

3. Clearing and cleaning, removing any large stones and roots of trees that have been left in the ground.

4. Seeding, using two bushels to the acre.

5. Light harrowing to cover the seed about one half inch.

6. Seeding again at two bushels to the acre, travelling at right angles to the first seeding.

7. Light harrowing to one half inch depth.

8. Rolling with not less than three hundred pounds' pressure.

After the ploughing, and before any other operation is begun, is the right time to mark the courses for roads and paths which can be laid off on the ground by means of stakes, and excavated. The advantage of attending to that detail at this time is this: the soil can be easily taken up, as it is loose and does not have to be broken apart, and it will be available for filling in any hollows or particularly deep places that have not been sufficiently filled in in the grading process.

Of course if the grading has been perfectly done there will be no such fills necessary, but in actual practice it usually happens that there are some depressions that had better be modified.

On the other hand, if the soil is not needed in that way, it can be evenly distributed over the rest of the surface, thus adding to the depth of available top soil; or, if the whole construction work is being carried on at one time, it can be deposited in the sites where the flower borders or shrubberies are to be planted. The ideal method, however, is to have the larger plantings done before the seeding of the lawn, thus avoiding traffic over the surface before the grass becomes established.

LEVELLING MADE EASY

The eye cannot be trusted to make perfect levels. It will inevitably, and quite unconsciously, seek to adjust the surface of the lawn in such a way as to make a generally harmonious contour with the general run of the ground. Therefore some mechanical means must be adopted to secure the perfect level.

The practical way, when there is no engineer or landscape architect engaged, is to drive stakes here and there in the ground, and sight from any one to a third stake by balancing a carpenter's level on the top of stake number one. By carrying this out over a series of three stakes in various directions, using each stake in turn as a support for the instrument, a perfect level can be assured. When once a stake has been driven or raised to the requisite height, it should be marked with paint, and it should remain in position until the final steps of the ground preparation are complete. By using a straight edged stiff board that will not sag, balancing it between two stakes, the ground can be brought up or cut down to the requisite level; and the intervening spaces may be filled in and levelled either by means of working a board over the surface in the same way as plasterers or masons work or by relying on the eye and using a rake.

Another method is by using the spirit level and theodolite, when stakes can be driven at various points and the height of a fill indicated by marking on the side of a stick the height of the future level. Where soil is to be removed a hole is dug and a stake inserted at its bottom is sunk to the right level. A distinct scheme of marking should be adopted, a common practice being to paint the top of such a stake with red.

FILLING AROUND TREES

Any specimen trees with well developed trunks should be retained so far as practicable. The effect of well-established specimens around the home is worth a great deal of effort to retain them. If only of moderate size it will possibly be better to raise them bodily, doing the work preferably in the winter time when the ball is frozen, after making the necessary provision for it in advance.

With old trees, or with those that are indigenous, not nursery grown, the risk involved in disturbing the roots is often too great. In such cases it will be better to leave them in situ and protect the base of the trunk from actual contact with the filled in earth. By no means bury the ball. Build up around the base of the trees with stones loosely piled one upon the other so that the air can have free access. If possible make this stone cylinder clear of the trunk by some few inches. A wall of this type (see Plate xv) will in nearly every instance preserve the tree in its normal health. In the case of a tree interfering with the slope of a terrace, the same method should be employed making the stone wall, however, only on the side where it is necessary to retain the earth (Plate xv).

UNDERDRAINAGE It is useless to attempt making a lawn on a site that is so wet that it holds water in pools after a rain. Wherever these conditions are encountered a system of underdrainage must be put in. The matter of tile draining is not properly a detail of lawn construction, however, for it should be given attention in all parts of estate construction. Drainage has the effect of improving the fertility of the soil by making it warmer, which also causes vegetation to start earlier in the spring. From these points alone it is a very essential detail in all garden work. The bright green appear-

All sites, unless exceptionally dry, are improved by drainage; it makes the soil warmer and growth starts earlier in spring

On steep slopes or terraces turf can be fastened by pegs or slats until they get established (see Plate XIV). Or deep rooting grasses may be sown

DRAINING AND TERRACING ance of the early lawn is particularly gratifying.

All heavy, cold soils will be improved by underdraining. In general, on lands which need drainage, tile should be laid three to six feet deep and at a distance of six to fifteen feet apart. There can be no absolute rule for the number of drains necessary. It is possible to over drain, but this is a result that is not likely to occur on a majority of soils. Sandy and very light leachy soils do not usually need drainage.

The drain ditch should be dug by a special draining spade which is very long and narrow, and care must be taken that the whole system of tiles runs on a gentle uniform slope to the lowest portion of the estate or to any other point where there is a suitable outlet. Drain tiles are of various sizes, and the smaller (two inch) tile should be used for the secondary or branch drains, larger ones being employed for the main courses.

A decision should be taken in the question of drainage at the very first, so as to allow time for the proper settling of the soil in the trenches. Six months before sowing the grass seed is none too soon.

Very often it is necessary to bring from a distance good top soil for the purpose of filling in hollows or for improving the natural soil of the site so as to get a sufficient depth for the grass roots. Inasmuch as different grasses have likings for different soils, it will readily be seen that the perfect lawn must consist of a uniform soil.

When importing top soil from a distance there is great danger of unevenness in the growth of the grasses on the future lawn unless precautions are taken to insure this uniformity of surface. No matter what soil you are dealing with, it is far better to thinly spread the additions over the entire surface rather than to fill in patches.

Where a rich top soil is being introduced from another source and there is a sufficient quantity available to make the entire lawn from the new soil, there will be no necessity to more than loosen the original. Therefore grading should be roughly finished before the new soil is introduced.

Where the supplies are being drawn from various different sources, bring in the heavier soil first, finishing off with the lighter, finer, and more friable. The only remedy for a patchy lawn, one part being on clay and the other part on sand, is to turn under the entire sod and start remaking the lawn.

The danger in imported soil when drawn from unknown sources lies in the possibility I had better indeed say probability of its containing weed seeds, which, worse still, would be different in the different lots of soil.

CHAPTER IV WHICH is BETTER: TURF OR SEED?

Two methods of lawn making Early advantages from turf Why seed is preferred Facts against turfing A comparison of costs When to sow Thick or thin seeding? How to broadcast Making terraces.

THERE are two methods by which a lawn may be established, by turf or by seed. As to which of these shall be adopted must be decided by the special circumstances in each case. By far the greater number of lawns are made from seed for the very good reason that the cost is'so much less than when turf is used. In fact on a question of cost there is absolutely no room for comparison. The preliminary preparation of the ground in either case must be the same, and the five dollars that would purchase a sufficiency of seed for one acre would go a very small way in the purchase of turves, which cost generally about eight cents a square foot.

ADVANTAGES OF TURF

The advantages of turf are these: that by securing turf from a lawn of known quality

32 IN THE SOD NURSERY

A practical method of lawn maintenance on large estates. Grow sods in an out-of-the-way place to have a supply ready to repair the formal lawn

REPAIRING WITH TURF

The best way to mend worn spots. Remove the old turf, making straight edges; loosen the soil and add a little fresh loam. Lay the new turf, fitting it osely and pound well so as to make a good union with the soil. Then water you can (provided your soil condition is right) reproduce a lawn of a given grass. Secondly and this is by far the greater advantage you get an immediate effect which is sometimes worth the extra expenditure of money, especially surrounding a house. For narrow borders of grass between the walks and flower beds turf is desirable. It is also the proper way of marking the boundaries of a newly laid out piece of ground before seeding. Turfing the edges assures a true line, and the seeding of the body can be done more thoroughly.

Sometimes it becomes desirable to make a lawn in the summer time, in which case it is far better to rely on laid sods. If cut and relaid with as little delay as possible on properly prepared ground the surface being raked loosely so as to assure immediate contact with the roots it will surely grow. Turf can be laid at any time when the ground can be worked, and is invaluable in that respect where cost is not a consideration. It is understood, however, that in all such cases, it must be watered persistently and a lawn made thus will need for the first twelve months of its existence a great deal more attention than one made from seed in the ordinary way.

FACTS AGAINST TURFING

Though turf will give immediate effect the seeded lawn will be every bit as satisfactory twelve months later, and in a great many cases it will be greatly superior. One great practical disadvantage to laid sod is the impossibility of making absolute unions between the turves. It is always necessary to fill in with good loam, sprinkling over it a little lawn grass mixture. When this germinates, there is a possibility of different grasses securing the early foot-hold, with a result that the entire surface of the lawn is marked out with a series of lines forming rectangular patterns.

It is difficult to obtain really good sod in any quantity. As a rule it is not for sale, but it can occasionally be secured as a consequence of the breaking up of some old estate. Even if in such a case you can get the sod for nothing, the expense of cutting, lifting, carting, and finally the relaying and beating down will be very great.

Where turf is laid on a heavy soil the effects of winter heaving are likely to be very marked; and if the lawn is laid in the spring and it is not abundantly watered all through the summer, it is certain that the drying out will result in gaping channels all over the surface. As a rule it will take two or three years before a laid lawn will assume the absolute uniformity of colour and texture that comes from thick seeding, and which is the ideal.

Sods are generally cut for convenience's sake three feet long and one foot wide, and in quantity can usually be bought at twenty cents a turf. I know of one man who has developed the regular business of growing sods for sale. His trade is in a city that is famous for its well kept gardens. He uses only the highest grade lawn mixture for raising of his crop which is given careful attention from first to last and he gets ten cents per square foot, thus realizing a profit of between five and six hundred dollars to the acre every three years. No turfs are cut and sold under that age. This is necessary, in fact, because the Kentucky blue grass will not have made a proper growth before this time. Turf raised thus, and sold locally, would make a better lawn than the average turf that is offered elsewhere, because the old and new soil conditions would be nearly identical, and the seeded-over portions would very quickly develop a very similar grass to that which was bought in the turf.

On well kept larger, private estates it is a common practice to grow turves in some out of the way corner so as to have a supply available for patching up or repairing any worn places that occur on the lawn in close proximity to the residence.

A COMPARISON OF COSTS

The average workman can lay in a day and do it perfectly about five or six hundred square feet of sod, giving thorough attention to levelling and making complete union. An expert can cover as much as eight hundred square feet or more. This is not work that can ordinarily be done by a common day labourer, and will generally cost two dollars a day. The cost for laying an acre at this rate would therefore be about one hundred and sixty dollars. Compare this with the cost of seeding. To begin with lawn grass seed at four bushels to the acre which is the proper quantity, will cost from twenty-to twenty-five dollars. The sowing can be done by one man in half a day at a cost of certainly not more than one dollar. Putting all these facts together, and bearing in mind that in two years there will not be anything to choose between the lawns, is it worth while to bother with sods? The cost of the preliminary preparations for seeding or sodding will not amount to less than seven and a half dollars for one acre. Ploughing can be done by one man in one day, and a team should be procurable under ordinary conditions for five dollars. Harrowing can be done in half a day. This figure is based upon the assumption that there is good land available. Subsoiling will add another five dollars and any extra work in the preparation, such as cleaning, the removal of tree stumps, rocks, etc., would have to be estimated for specially.

LAYING SODS

Two men are necessary to handle turves, both in the cutting and in the laying, whereas one man can do the sowing. A large turf is superior to a small one because there will be fewer joints when dealing with the larger pieces. But it is not practicable to handle them in larger sizes than 3 x I feet. There is a special tool made for taking up the turves known as a turfing iron. This is essentially a long-shafted spade with a thin, flat blade which can be pushed under the turf, cutting the roots and leaving the flat sod ready to be rolled. Generally a common spade is used, two men working together, the one rolling the turf as it is cut by the other man.

When relaying on the new ground the turf is unrolled in position, any little unevenness of the ground or of the thickness of the turf being repaired as the work proceeds. It is not easy to make a perfectly level surface. A slight difference in the compactness of the roots of the grasses in the turf will lead to hollows and hummocks in the near future, which have to be filled up by additions of soil above or under the turf; or the hummocks have to be beaten down by means of a heavy piece of wood fixed to a handle at a suitable angle (like a broom), or the back of a spade is used. The latter is the more likely, not because it is the best but because it is the most handy.

After the turf is laid as evenly as possible, and the unions filled with fresh soil, there comes the very essential work of beating. This is really hard work. The turves must be beaten and pounded down to ensure intimate contact with the soil below. If this is not done the roots fail to take hold and the grasses die after a few days of dry, hot weather. Watering will help a great deal, and should be done all summer on a newly laid turf lawn.

On terraces and banks sods are better than seed, because they can be fixed in position by means of pegs eight or ten inches long driven into the ground. If there is not enough turf of the right kind to dress the bank completely, small pieces may be planted as "cuttings" and seed sown on the spaces between or around. Terraces are prone to dry out in summer and the turf method is calculated to overcome this tendency to loss.

WHEN TO SOW In the greater part of the country where lawns are maintained, that is in the entire temperate zone, there are two periods of the year when new lawns may be successfully seeded April to May, and again in September. There is no best date for sowing. In the Northern States September and November are generally preferred because the risk of sudden drying out by excessively hot weather after the seeds germinate is avoided. In the Southern States November sees the greatest amount of seeding. When seeding is done in the spring it is usually, according to location, sometime between February and May, the earlier date of course referring to the South.

The point in spring seeding is to get it done as soon as possible after the ground is in workable condition. I have seen lawns successfully sown in June and even in July, but the practice is not to be generally recommended as in the majority of cases, and with the majority of people, failure would result.

If it is inconvenient to sow the lawn in the fall it is a good practice to have the ground thoroughly prepared then and seed at any time during the winter. If the seed is scattered over the surface of the snow it will be washed into the earth when the thaws come and brought into such intimate contact with the soil that its early germination and perfect stand is a foregone conclusion. On very wet soils seeding in the summer time is advisable.

For summer seeding, oats at the rate of one quart to three hundred may be added to the regular lawn grass mixture. This grass germinates very quickly and endures the hot weather well. It will act as a "nurse" to the other grasses which will be thus encouraged to make a growth. The oats will not interfere with the lawn grasses and they are killed entirely by the cutting of the mower, which prevents their seeding. So marked is the nursing effect of oats that it is a valuable addition at any time when sowing a lawn mixture on banks or terraces. Its quick root development assists greatly in holding the soil until the permanent grasses come into possession. This is a practical method of obviating the necessity of turfing on terraces.

THE ART OF SOWING

Lawn grass seed is sown broadcast. It must be evenly distributed over the entire surface of the ground, and at the rate of not less than four bushels to the acre. For smaller areas allow one quart of seed to three-hundred square feet.

Select a quiet day for the work of seeding. Don't be tempted to hurry, and, if the day selected should turn out to be windy, postpone the operation. The grass seed is so fine and so easily caught by the wind that an even distribution becomes impossible if the day be not quiet. A very slight wind will do no harm, but there must not be enough movement to carry the fine seed away from the area directly under the hand; otherwise the mixtures will be separated.

When sowing keep the hand low, stoop down and taking a handful of seed with the fingers of the hands lightly bent and slightly separated let the arm swing freely in a semicircle so as to scatter the seed well and evenly. A reference to Plate vi will enable the reader to form some idea of the correct and incorrect methods of seeding.

THICK OR THIN SEEDING?

It is better to sow thickly than to be sparing of the seed for the simple reason that the weeds have less chance to take hold of the ground if it is abundantly occupied by the grass plants. Another advantage is that the crowding of the plants results in a finer leaf, which is often very desirable. Seed is far cheaper than the labour that would be involved in digging out the weeds later on. A more even distribution of seed is made by going over the ground twice, using one half the quantity each time, and making the tracks of the second seeding at right angles with those of the first. Broadcast the seed as you walk up and down the whole patch until it has been completely covered, making parallel tracks. Immediately after the seed is sown the whole area should be lightly harrowed or raked so as to just cover the seed. Then roll. Do this after each seeding and finish off with a heavy roller, weighing not less than three hundred pounds if possible, to make the surface compact and to insure a thorough contact of the seed and the soil. Firming of the soil means good germination of the seed.

On the new lawn Rolling the keynote of success Winter heaving Springtime repairs Mowing essential How often to cut The clippings Effects of insufficient cutting Weather conditions When to mow and water The fallacy of sprinkling How to use the hose.

ROLLING, mowing, and watering are the three essential details which require attention every year, and they must be carried out thoroughly year after year, without any sort of lessened vigour because the lawn is established. The whole object and aim of the after attention is to secure a uniform sod and even texture over the entire surface of the lawn.

ATTENTION THE FIRST YEAR

A fall-sown lawn will hardly stand in need of mowing the same season. If the seeding was done in the spring or summer the grass must be cut as soon as it has attained a height

PLATE XTII

STEPPING A SLOPE

This prevents washing during heavy rains, makes walking easier, and looks well far better than a worn track!

of about three inches. But don't be in a hurry over this first trim. Use a scythe by preference. You will not then cut too close to the roots. Leave the cut grass on the lawn to act as a mulch.

After the grass has commenced to grow freely it may be cut once in ten days, and also rolled. In its first season the grass will not be rooted very firmly and the pulling of the knives of the average lawn mower will not tend to help things along. If a lawn mower is used see to it that the knives are set high, and keep the grass about two inches long all the season. In extreme hot weather the cutting may be lighter; rolling would be of more service.

The new lawn needs rolling frequently to make the roots as firm as possible, and the heavier the roller, the better. One man cannot be expected to haul a roller heavier than three hundred pounds, but a thousand-pound machine would be none too heavy.

As the fall approaches the mowing machine may be set to cut closer than it was in the summer, but cutting must cease for the year about the middle of September.

Nothing conduces more to the maintenance of perfect condition in the lawn than persistent and early rolling each year; not that rolling should be omitted any time during the season, but it is especially necessary in the early spring. Just as soon as the ground becomes workable and the grass starts into growth the whole surface should be thoroughly rolled again and again to effectively overcome the loosening effects of the freezing and thawing of winter.

The heavier the land, as a rule, the more necessary does rolling become. Everyone is familiar with the manner in which the plants in the herbaceous border are heaved out of the ground by the alternate thawing and freezing of winter. It is also one of the most potent sources of trouble in the strawberry patch, and is one of the strongest arguments advanced against fall planting. The same thing happens to the grass plants, the opening of heavy soils is persistent and continuous, and will play havoc even with a well made lawn unless persistent steps be taken each spring to counteract it.

Top dressings of good garden loam rich fertiliser is not indicated and rolling again and again will accomplish wonders. It is hardly possible to make the surface of the lawn too compact by this process. A roller which will exert a pressure of a thousand or even fifteen hundred pounds will not be too heavy. Therefore use as heavy a piece of machinery as you can comfortably handle. What is known as the water ballast roller, which consists of two hollow cylinders into which water or sand can be poured to ballast and attain the necessary weight, should find a place in the equipment of every country estate where a lawn of any large dimensions is to be maintained in good condition. These rollers are made on what is called the sectional pattern, that is, they consist of two or three distinct cylinders by means of which the machine can be turned without tearing the surface of the lawn; the two sections operate in different directions.

WHEN TO MOW

Mowing is necessary inasmuch as it prevents the plants from going to seed; and the prevention of seeding encourages vigorous vegetative growth, which means abundant foliage and bright healthy green colour. Nothing will work greater injury than seed formation. It exhausts the plant, and with many of the grasses which are included in lawn mixtures will inevitably result in their dying out.

If a lawn mower of the ordinary rotary knife type is used there is a tendency (especially in the younger age of the lawn) to set the knives so as to cut too close to the ground. This is trying in a variety of ways. Depriving the plant of nearly all its foliage taxes its vitality until it shall have made another start. In the meantime, as frequently happens in the early days of spring, there is a likelihood of the weather becoming suddenly hot and dry. The surface of the ground being exposed to the direct action of the sun's rays, and especially if there has been any large degree of feeding during the winter, the tax on the plants' constitution, as may be easily realised, is very severe. It is quite possible, indeed, to burn out some of the grasses in this way in the very earliest days of spring.

But frequent mowing is necessary owing to the vigorous growth that the grass will make, and it is generally better to mow often, say once a week, with the knives set high, than it is to allow the grass to attain several inches and then with a low set mower, to cut it right down close to the ground. It is a mistake to set apart a definite day for mowing, and then do the work because it is on the schedule. One must be guided by conditions, and if growth is very rapid mowing becomes necessary at very short intervals.

In general the knives should not be set less than two inches high, especially on lawns which are subject to traffic or usage of any sort. But if the grass has been allowed to get very long, the cutting should not be so close at first, and it would be better to use a scythe.

On areas of grass close around the house, on tennis lawns, and as edgings to flower beds or shrubbery groups bordering walks and drive ways, persistent cutting, and maintaining the grass as near as possible at one uniform height throughout the year, conduces immensely to the general tone of neatness of the entire establishment. A garden where these features receive attention only occasionally, at somewhat lengthy intervals, looks irregular at all times, and when a great length of grass is removed, exposing the lower more or less yellowish under-texture, there is an unpleasant alternation of ragged long green and short yellowish brown. Of course if clover has been used freely in the mixture, and if some of the fescues are growing, the yellow effect of a closely cut lawn is not apparent, that is, so long as these maintain their hold on the ground. But in a properly prepared soil and a properly managed lawn they will be eventually crowded out as the permanent grasses gain control.

LEAVE OR REMOVE THE CLIPPINGS?

The clippings from the use of the lawn mower may, generally, be left on the surface of the lawn, not raked off. If the lawn be given constant attention, and cut whenever it needs it, so as to keep it as uniformly as possible at a height of about two inches, the clippings cannot be considered as an objection. Very often indeed they are positively beneficial, as they act as a mulch to the newly exposed soil. If a suddenly hot spell follows upon the cutting time the advantage of this slight protection to the soil is considerable.

If the grass has been allowed to grow to a considerable length, it will be necessary to rake off the clippings, and especially so if the soil is moist and very rich, because the cut grass will hang too heavily about the roots, and rotting, will give origin to a good deal of trouble.

On very poor soils it may be advisable to leave the clippings even if they are long. Rest assured that they will never be detrimental to the lawn unless they produce an unsightly effect. The cut grass will soon wither in the hot sun, and a few hours after the lawn mower has been taken over the surface there will be very little trace of the clippings.

THE IDEAL MOWING DAY

Select a dull, cloudy day for mowing, if possible. The grass will cut more easily, and if it is to be raked off after clipping it is more easy to handle, and the shock to the plant from the cut surfaces is considerably less on a day when the sun does not strike with all its force.

But watering, when it becomes necessary on account of excessive drought, should be attended to independently of the weather. Of course there will be some loss from surface evaporation, if watering be done on a dry hot soil while the sun is still brightly shining, but it is an infinitesimal fraction and not worth serious consideration, and the benefit done to the grass will far offset any such loss.

THE FALLACY OF SPRINKLING

Too often, because it is easier in the after years of the lawn's existence, the only attention it gets, other than occasional mowing, is watering; and this watering is generally accomplished in the most haphazard and laziest form imaginable. Surface sprinkling is responsible for more ultimate damage to otherwise good lawns than most people, perhaps, imagine. It is a very common practice to connect the sprinkler to the water stand-pipe, place it in the middle of the lawn, and let the water play for a few hours of an evening. It looks so pretty with the jets of fine spray glistening in the evening sun! It makes a great show but accomplishes precious little. Far better would it be to give the lawn a thorough soaking with water straight out from the nozzle of a hose once a week, or even once in two or three weeks. When you do water, water thoroughly.

Light surface sprinklings accomplish this much of good: They do check transpiration from the leaves and evaporation from the surface of the ground for a short time. But the trouble is that they do not give enough water to soak into the ground and really saturate it for a depth of some inches. The roots of the plants show a very natural tendency to seek the best supply of moisture, and continuous light surface sprinklings have the result of drawing the roots to the surface whereas they should properly be penetrating deep into the lower layers of the soil. This of course is but another argument for the very thorough and very deep preliminary preparation of the site. If the roots can find all they require at a depth of eight inches to a foot below the surface rest assured they will travel down to it. A lawn thus prepared in the first place can withstand the trials of an ordinary summer in the eastern United States without being watered even once, provided always that the site is not unduly drained, nor on the slope of a hill exposed to peculiarly drying conditions.

Occasionally there will be exceptional seasons which must be met by exceptional actions. Watering may then be a prime necessity, but as a rule if the beginnings are properly made, watering is not a necessity on the lawn. How much better to spend another twelve or twenty-five dollars an acre in the beginning, and avoid the mental worry, the continuous labour, and the unwelcome water bills of later years!

Even on sandy soils watering can be to a great extent obviated, and it is folly on any sort of soil to rush to use the hose in the early part of the year. On small lawns, watering is not such a serious problem; and, especially where the foundation has been on the inert soil thrown out in making the foundations for the house, it may not be economically practical to take the preliminary steps which would avoid its necessity. But on large areas of even half an acre the question of summer maintenance may become a seriously expensive problem.

When watering is necessary let it be done by laying the hose on the ground and allowing the water to flow freely from it in one spot for about an hour. Then move the end of the hose to another spot, thus watering the lawn in sections, the edges of which will just overlap. This can be carried on all day long, and at night too, for that matter. There is no reason whatever why the lawn should not be watered in the day time, sunshine notwithstanding. Even though it did result in burning in a few instances through the drops of water focusing the rays of the sun on to the leaves, the damage done will not be any more noticeable than is the browning of the cut edges which results from the use of the lawn mower.

CHAPTER VI How TO FEED A LAWN

Making a good start Green manure and humus Artificial fertilisers Dressing the new lawn Keeping old lawns up to pitch Top dressings Animal manure vs. chemical fertilisers Where weeds come from Stable manure Sheep manure Wood ashes Bone-meal Nitrate of soda Top dressings Lime for sour soils Tobacco stems.

NOBODY expects good corn from unfed land. It is a matter of good gardening to feed the land heavily for all the vegetable crops. Yet they are cleared annually, and the ground has the benefit of cultivation while they are growing. But the lawn is too often neglected. The grass is a permanent crop and really needs richer feeding than many of the vegetable crops. The ground cannot be cultivated after the grass is growing, but it can, and must, be thoroughly enriched before. Manure ploughed under at the time of the general preparation is the foundation for later feeding with chemical fertilisers.

On sandy soils the dressing of manure can be much heavier than on heavy soils, and will 56 In the winter time, after the ground is frozen and when it will support traffic, manure may be hauled on to the lawn and spread over the snow

A top dressing of fine, short manure may be scattered over the grass in earliest spring, before the trees leaf. Make board tracks for the wheelbarrow

TWO METHODS OF FEEDING be more economical than artificial fertilisers, which will leach out. On heavy soils a chemical fertiliser will answer. The objection to the use of stable manure is the risk of carrying in weed seeds, which can only be avoided by seeing that the manure is well rotted. The proper quality is not easy to get, and rather than run any risk it would be better to rely on turning under a green crop to supply the humus. This may he accomplished by sowing either cowpeas or crimson clover. Ground bone (3,000 pounds to the acre) may then be mixed in when harrowing and raking, and, if there is a tendency to acidity, add lime.

Another formula that has given satisfaction is:

Lime superphosphate 2 cwt.

Guano I cwt.

Bone meal I cwt.

Never add pure chemical fertilisers to the ground just before seeding. There can be but one result the loss of the seed. If the plant food has not been added a month before sowing time wait until the grass is well up.

DRESSING THE NEW LAWN

Very well rotted manure can be put on the new lawn as a fall mulch, as much to keep the roots of the new lawn in proper condition over the first winter as for any food value it may have. In parts of the country where tobacco stems are easily obtainable from factories, they should be used in preference. They are cleaner, they cannot carry weed seeds, and the insecticidal properties of the tobacco juices are of some importance.

Sheep manure, using about one ton to the acre, will be found thoroughly satisfactory, and will not cause damage by bringing in weeds. For my own part I object to disfiguring the lawn with this sort of material, unless it be needed as a mulch. If for feeding, I would rely upon chemical fertilisers. The manures give nitrogen, which is more conveniently applied in the form of soda nitrate at the rate of 200 pounds to the acre. It must be scattered just in advance of a rain, or applied in liquid form, using one pound to forty gallons of water.

If the beginning has been throughly and conscientiously done, that is, if the soil is properly prepared in the first place and properly enriched at the rate of twenty-five hundred pounds of well rotted stable manure to the acre or an equivalent in ground bone and wood ashes, there should be no necessity for adding fertiliser to the lawn for, perhaps, ten years after its establishment unless the land is extremely porous. Where this has not been done, however, feeding will have to begin possibly the very first year. It should never be forgotten that grass is feeding on the ground continuously and that it is being continuously cut.

After the lawn is made, it is impossible, of course, to treat it in the same way as you treat the tilled area of the garden or the borders. In both these cases when fertility is to be increased it can be accomplished by spreading over the surface a dressing of organic manure and spading it under. In the very nature of things such a course is out of the question as regards the lawn. There top dressings of easily soluble fertilisers are necessary. Even the surface of the grass must not be interfered with, it must not be buried, and the lawn must remain in service.

MANURING IN WINTER If stable manure is to be used at all it should preferably be carried on to the lawn some time during the winter. An excellent plan is to wait until the ground is frozen and partially covered with snow when a horse and wagon may be drawn across its surface without any permanent injury accruing. At other times of the year there is danger of furrowing the lawn by the wheels of the wagon; should this happen during the winter it is of no great moment, as the damage can be easily repaired in the early spring by filling in with top soil and reseeding as necessary.

When stable manure is used it must be what is spoken of as "well rotted." Fresh manure will always import weed seeds. The damage that thus may be done to the lawn in one season may take two or three years of constant vigilance to reduce. If assured that there are no live weed seeds contained in it stable manure is the best sort of top dressing that can be put on to the lawn aside from its ugliness! If spread over in the early winter and left until the grass begins to grow vigorously in the spring it will have served a dual purpose. Not only has the lawn received the benefit of its fertilising qualities, but the service of the mulch in modifying the effects of the alternate freezing and thawing will have been extremely beneficial. In the early spring rake the coarse material from the lawn and then go over the surface with a heavy roller.

WEEDS AND ORGANIC MANURES

The objection to ordinary stable manure being used as a top dressing on the lawn does not apply to the other animal manures inasmuch as they do not contain weed seeds. Of these possible substitutes, however, the only one that can be recommended for general use is sheep manure. This is a highly concentrated fertiliser, and contains a very small amount of water. It is weight for weight the richest manure produced by any of the common farm animals. It decomposes rapidly and loses a large proportion of its ammonia (nitrogen). This would be obviated by composting with earth or land plaster in the proportion of two parts manure to one of the earth or plaster.

As offered commercially dry sheep manure may be used as a dressing for the lawn at the rate of one half ton, to one ton, per acre. It will possibly be more efficient when used in spring, as in that way the full benefit of the nitrogen would be retained, but it may be also used as a fall dressing. The disadvantage of using animal manures for top dressing in the spring is that the bright green appearance of the lawn which is one of the most pleasing effects of the spring landscape is seriously marred. It is sometimes stated that clover seeds are imported with sheep manure. If this be so it is not a very serious objection. On the other hand it should be remembered that the ordinary commercial sheep manure is what is known as "kiln-dried and pulverised," in which case of course, even if there were live clover seeds in the natural product, they would be destroyed in the preparation and handling.

SPRING TOP DRESSINGS

As a spring top dressing finely ground bone meal and sifted wood ashes, in equal parts by weight, should be distributed over the surface of the lawn at the rate of one ton to the acre. This would mean a distribution over the surface about as thick as would give an even covering, leaving the lawn with a slightly grayish colour. This top dressing may safely be used in heavier doses than the uninitiated would imagine. It is better to select for the broadcasting a day when rain is anticipated so that the fertiliser may be washed down to the roots of the grass at once.

Nitrate of soda as a top dressing is used broadcast up to five hundred pounds per acre. It would be better to apply this quantity in two or even three separate dressings rather than all at once. Nitrate of soda is so easily soluble in water that even moderate rains on a well drained and especially on a leechy soil will wash away the greater part of a heavy dressing, which is thus utterly lost. If this is scattered over the surface on a dry day, and is not quickly followed by rain, the grass will inevitably be burned because the salt will extract water from the foliage of the grasses. To avoid this, some people prefer to apply nitrate of soda in a solution, and it may be prepared at the rate of one pound in forty gallons of water. The effect of nitrate of soda is very rapid. The grass will be seen to respond immediately to the application, it will make a vigorous growth and assume a richer, deeper green colour, the result being especially marked on light soils.

This top dressing may be used at any time during the season when it is desirable to force a quick growth in spots that have become bare through usage, and in certain cases it is better to rely upon it than to fall back on reseeding, as for instance when the bareness is due to heavy traffic. Reseeding in such a case would not be effectual, because the young plants would be trampled to death as soon as they are germinated. On the other hand, nitrate of soda may be regarded as a forcing or stimulating food and should always be supplemented with something of a more lasting character and which will assist the plants in building up a hardy and vigorous structure.

LONG LASTING FERTILISERS

Of the more permanent fertilisers bone meal and hard wood ashes are the best. The former, for top dressing, must be used in what is known as fine meal. The coarse ground bone takes too long to dissolve and comes in too large particles for convenient use. Raw crushed bone is to be used only in the original preparation of the ground. Bone meal acts slowly but a dressing once a year at the rate of five hundred pounds to the acre will give marvellous returns. It can be used at any time, and on very light, sandy soils it is common practice to apply a top dressing in the late summertime.

Phosphates are particularly beneficial in giving vigour to grass plants. They may be applied better by means of bone meal than by any of the chemical fertilisers. Bone meal also contains a fair proportion of slowly available nitrogen, and where there is no need for special sudden stimulation it may be used to the exclusion of nitrate of soda or animal manures.

WOOD ASHES AND LIME

Hardwood ashes, broadcasted at the rate of one ton to the acre, are peculiarly available on blue grass lawns inasmuch as they carry with them a quantity of lime which will neutralise any tendency to acidity in the soil, thus making it a more congenial medium for the Kentucky blue grass.

Lime itself is indicated as a winter dressing and can be used at the rate of forty bushels to the acre or roughly speaking, one bushel per thousand square feet or two handfuls to the square yard. As Kentucky blue grass forms the basis of the standard lawn mixtures, and is the one grass which it is hoped will ultimately occupy the entire area to the exclusion of all others which were there in the beginning, an annual dressing of lime may safely be given. This is preferably spread over the ground some time in the winter after it has been frozen. Lime to be used on the lawn should be air slaked.

A practical method of procuring a supply for the suburban gardener is to purchase quick lime by the barrel in the early spring and have it stored in barrels or boxes in the cellar until it is to be used. It will in this way serve two purposes. In the process of air slaking, which goes on throughout the summer, it will absorb moisture from the air and to a considerable extent will aid in drying the cellar. By fall it will be thoroughly slaked and ready for use. This annual dressing will largely help in eradicating moss and sorrel or sour grass, which invariably take possession of sour soils.

Tobacco leaf stems and tobacco stalks are used as a mulch for winter in districts where they are readily available. Spread over the lawn they serve to protect it from the action of frost and have some slight influence in controlling insects. They cannot be said to act greatly as a fertiliser although there is a common belief to that effect. If spread over in the fall they will usually have rotted by spring, and there is little coarse material to be gathered up.

No room for weeds on a well kept lawn Guarding against infection The commonest pests Digging out dandelions and plantains Poisoning the root Sour grass and moss Lime the remedy The pestiferous crab-grass The friendly frost Bermuda grass in the North Fall grasses Fall weeding best Poultry manure vs. weeds Ants The white grub Earthworms Moles Fairy rings and other fungi.

UNLESS a lawn is maintained in its highest efficiency, and the growth of the grass continuously stimulated, weeds will creep in. The surest method of keeping out the undesirable growths among the grass is by keeping the good growth thoroughly occupying the ground. As sure as the desirable lawn grasses are allowed to die out, undesirable, rank growing weeds will immediately occupy the ground nature abhors a blank spot.

Where such weeds have secured a foothold, they should be dug out by one of the convenient hand tools, going over the ground most thoroughly in the spring time and persisting

What happens if the dandelions are not cut out! The bright yellow flowers are very pretty, but they will develop seeds

The result of neglect. Note how the plantains have taken possession of the portion that was not reseeded. Oust weeds by growing grass!

LESSONS WITH WEEDS in the work as long as the plants show any tendency to active growth, and on no account must they be allowed to run to seed. So far as possible neighbouring uncultivated patches which have become a prey to common weeds should be roughly mowed over with the scythe two or three times during the year, or they may be burnt over. In fact almost any means is justifiable in order to reduce the chances of infection by weed seeds. The most common pests of the lawn are the dandelion, the plantains, dock, crab-grass, Bermuda grass (in northern lawns) wild carrot, chickweed, sorrel, and moss.

DIG OUT THESE WEEDS

The dandelions, plantains, and dock must be cut out, root and all. It is no good to merely crop off the rosette of leaves without digging in to the soil and taking out as much of the root as possible. Indeed, very often the mere chopping off of the rosette will result in an increase of the number of crowns later in the season. In the early spring time, in many parts of the country, it is no uncommon thing to see itinerant Italians travel- ling from garden to garden digging up the dandelions which they sell in the cities for salad purposes. These scavengers should be encouraged. They save annually thous-sands of lawns from the presence of this weed. To a certain extent, it must be confessed that dandelions and daisies are pretty adjuncts to the grass plot. The danger is, however, that they are likely to overwhelm the grass; and, moreover, though the golden flowers of the dandelion are pretty enough in all truth, yet the globular white seed balls are far from decorative. When digging the roots out of the lawn, the worker may at the same time repair the damage by treading the surface till the hole is closed. Where bad patches have occurred, resulting in ugly large sized holes, it will be better, however, to scatter over the surface a little good quality garden loam or soil from the compost heap, and finish off by scattering a pinch or two of lawn seed mixture, beating the surface well with the back of the spade.

Plantains are more easily dug out than dandelions. They cannot be made use of in any way, but they will seed very freely and soon become a pest on the untended lawn.

They show a great tendency to occupy soil of a somewhat heavy nature, especially one that is insufficiently drained. The work of removal should be accomplished in the early spring before the plants have come into flower. There are two species of plantain which are sufficiently well known, the one having narrow leaves six to seven inches long and half an inch wide, commonly called rib grass; the other having shorter, much wider leaves, strongly marked with the parallel veins or ribs. The plantains make a strong root, but do not penetrate so deeply as the dandelion. They throw out more lateral rootlets which are strong and wiry, and generally it is necessary to make a pretty wide cut in order to remove the plant properly.

If it is not convenient to cut out the entire root they may be killed, after the crown has been removed, by poison. A crystal of sulphate of iron, (green vitriol) placed on the top of the cut surface will dissolve and kill the root which is left behind. Such treatment, however, is not generally recommended, as there is danger of strong corrosive chemicals doing damage to the grass roots by spreading in solution in the soil and neces- skating very extensive repairs by turfing or reseeding. A drop or two of gasoline is said to be effective.

THE RESULT OF SOUR SOIL

Sour grass (or sorrel) and moss are pests on many lawns and are sure indicators of unsatisfactory ground conditions. The lawn which has become infested with these weeds is in all probability sour and badly drained. The easiest immediate remedy is by winter dressings of air slacked lime at the rate of one bushel to a thousand square feet of lawn. Better, however, it would be to underdrain by sinking lines of tile. Land can be over-drained, an extreme which must be avoided, and for which it is not possible to lay down any definite rules. It is a matter of judgment, and, generally, some good idea of the number of drain ditches that should be put in can be ascertained from some local farmer or gardener who has had experience with the soil of the locality. Bottom lands will always need more drainage than up-lands. The advantage of attacking these weeds by a surface dressing of lime is especially marked on a blue grass lawn as the grass will make a much more vigorous growth in the presence of the lime. It is possible, indeed, to maintain the lawn in very good average condition by annual dressings of lime in the quantity here advised.

THE WORST WEED OF ALL

Crab grass (Syntherisma or Panicum sangu'male is the worst weed enemy of the lawn. It creeps over the surface in such a way that it is untouched by the lawn mower, yet a strenuous fight must be waged against it as soon as its presence is recognised. It is an annual and will reseed itself year after year unless it is attacked and actually pulled out. The seeds germinate in June and early August and its unwelcome presence in the full summer season mars what may be otherwise a good lawn, by its broad pale green leaves, which give a very patchy and unhappy appearance to the general surface of the grass. As soon as the cold weather approaches the creeping stems of the crab grass change to a bronzy red colour, which becomes more and more intense as the cold increases, making the lawn in the latter part of the season look quite "rusty"; which no amount of watering will revive into bright green. The first touch of frost spells death to the crab grass, but there is little satisfaction to be derived from that fact. Where it is killed the lawn is left with unsightly brown patches which are open to the inroads of weeds and there is always the certainty that the plant has infected the lawn with its own seeds for another year's crop.

There is only one practical method of attack, and that is both costly and burdensome. As soon as the grass begins to spread, take a sharp-toothed garden rake and yank up the creeping stems of the crab grass, pulling them clear from the surface of the soil and leaving them spread on the top of the regular lawn surface. If the lawn mower with knives set very low be now run over the ground the flower heads will be cut off, which will prevent the seeding. If this is not done during June and July the low creeping stems will by the end of August have successfully crowded out and killed many of the more desirable grasses. It is no use to merely run the mower over the lawn without previously pulling up the creeping stems in the way de- scribed, for the machine will then simply cut the leaves, actually stimulating the stalks below to further growth and tighter rooting into the ground. Rollingwith a three-thousand-pound machine has killed crab grass in Philadelphia.

OTHER WEED GRASSES

Bermuda grass (Capriola, or Cynodon, Dac-tylori) is objectionable in Northern lawns merely because it becomes discoloured on the first touch of frost, leaving ugly brown patches. Of itself it is not otherwise undesirable. In a blue grass lawn this patchiness toward the end of the season is very undesirable, and the Bermuda grass may therefore be classed as a weed north of Washington. South of that city and especially upon the sandy soils of the Atlantic coast Bermuda grass is the main dependence for lawns.

As the fall approaches, orchard grass (Dactylis glomerata is likely to make its appearance in many lawns, so is timothy (Phleum pratense). They may even come in accidentally with low grade lawn mixtures. Wherever they appear they should be ruthlessly dug up; in fact no strong growing bunch or tuft grass should be tolerated for an instant. They should immediately be dug up, lawn grass seeds scattered on the bare spot, and the soil firmed down with the back of the spade.

WHEN TO DIG WEEDS It is better to dig out these rank growing weeds in the fall, rather than in the spring, as their removal in the early part of the year opens up a quickly-seized chance for crab grass to gain a foothold, especially during the hot weather which may be expected from the middle of May onward. Very often the regular grasses of the lawn are burned out about this time, and it is well not to give too much leeway for the crab grass which germinates in June. The lawn should be in better condition by the end of October than it was in April.

From time to time, varying in different parts of the country and on different soils, hosts of other plants will gain entry to the lawn as weeds, but the foregoing are the more common pests which occur generally. These other weeds have more or less shallow rooting and may generally be eradicated by encouraging a growth of the regular lawn grasses.

In other words the best way to keep out weeds is to keep in grass. The well maintained lawn which is properly cared for in the early spring and which receives an annual top dressing of some fertiliser as already described will not, under ordinary conditions and in ordinary seasons, be seriously menaced by weeds. When a wet, warm summer occurs many other plants may become very bothersome weeds. Chickweed may be taken as a sample. It will then overrun the grass, and must be raked out.

Clover is not generally regarded as undesirable on the lawn (indeed it is usually seeded over in order to get a quick green effect), and many people advocate its presence because its low growing foliage leaves the newly cut lawn with a fresh green colour which would not be the case if the bare stems of the grasses alone were seen. It grows below the level of the lawn mower as generally set, and does not interfere with the growth of the permanent grasses.

A USE FOR POULTRY

The suburban gardener who keeps poultry has at hand a very simple method of eradi- eating weeds from his lawn. The manure from the poultry house can be saved and composted and spread over the lawn in the fall. This can be put on as thickly as convenient and will have a very stimulating effect upon the growth of the grass in the spring; so strong will the growth be that the weeds will be crowded out of existence. Hen manure to be used in this way should be gathered daily during the season, mixed with an equal quantity of earth or plaster, and stored in a dry place until wanted for use. A dressing of a bushel to a thousand square feet of surface will not be excessive.

INSECTS THAT BOTHER MOST

Perhaps the most troublesome of the minor insects are the red and black ants. These are not usually serious pests on other than light dry sandy soils. With a properly prepared site, in which a due proportion of clay has been incorporated, ants will very rarely occur. The chief injury they render is by the manner in which they loosen up the soil around the roots of the grasses. They do not directly attack the plants themselves;

but, by loosening the ground in making their tunnels and galleries, the effect is that the roots become dried out and the tops naturally suffer.

The most effectual means of attack is to poison the ants by means of bisulphide of carbon. The work can be quickly accomplished and though not a particularly pleasant operation, it is not so objectionable that there is any excuse for avoiding it. The bisulphide of carbon is a heavy, colourless, volatile liquid which easily sinks into the ground, and the fumes, which are heavier than the air, quickly penetrate downward into the most remote corners of the ants' runs. One or two table-spoonfuls of the liquid may be carefully poured into the opening of the nest and a damp cloth or a handful of soil should be immediately put over it and packed down tightly. Nothing else is necessary. If one application does not entirely rid the lawn of these little pests, it is a simple matter to repeat the attack.

One word of caution is well in reference to the handling of this poison. It is highly inflammable, and the vapour is dangerously explosive. Be very careful, therefore, not to use bisulphide of carbon in the presence of a naked light, or in the neighbourhood of a fire.

It is sometimes recommended that, after pouring in the liquid and allowing it to vapour-ise a short time, the covering should be lifted and a match applied to explode the nests. While this may be done, and will be effective in killing the ants, yet it is entirely unnecessary and may even be detrimental to the general condition of the lawn otherwise, inasmuch as the shock of the explosion will aggravate the loosening of the soil around the roots. After the treatment with the bisulphide of carbon, say in the course of two or three hours, the lawn should be copiously watered after rolling with a heavy roller.

A similar treatment may be applied for any other insects that are found sneaking in the lawn.

The white grub of the June beetle will occasionally gain a foothold in untended lawns, especially those that are insufficiently mown. This pest burrows into the ground and feeds on the roots of the grasses, causing very serious damage and often resulting in the entire killing out of the plants. When patches of brown occur on a lawn in summer the pres- ence of the white grub may be suspected. These grubs live in the ground three years before emerging into the perfect insects. They may be brought under control by ploughing in fall and allowing chickens to forage on the lawn, as they are particularly fond of these fat grubs. On lawns which cannot be ploughed up, sprayings with kerosene emulsion has been found a good remedy. The use of a very heavy roller has often been satisfactory in crushing the grubs in light soils.

EARTH WORMS AND THEIR CASTS

Earth worms are an indication of an improperly drained top soil, or of a soil that is cold or heavy. They rarely occur in troublesome quantity on good mellow soils which are warm and abundantly underdrained. As a matter of fact, their presence would be taken as a very index to the fact that the soil lacks humus. They are nature's most efficient agents in transforming a cold tight soil which lacks humus, and is therefore somewhat unresponsive in cultivation, into a soil that is warmer and generally better adapted for plant growing. They are kept out of tennis courts by providing ample drainage some considerable distance below the surface by means of a layer of coal ashes for instance. They will not work up through such a material. If they are especially troublesome which will be manifested by the number of casts thrown up all over the surface of the lawn the best immediate remedy is to water with lime-water, made by dissolving lime and allowing the liquid to settle and clear. The upper portion may then be used through an ordinary watering can. If a good application of lime water is made in the evening when the work of the worms is especially troublesome, they will be drawn to the surface, and can be brushed or raked up early the next morning. Worm casts must be brushed off the lawn before rolling, otherwise the grass will be killed by the cakes of compact earth. Other suggestions for dealing with worm casts will be found in Chapter XIII.

THE MOLE

The most bothersome animal pest is the mole. Tunnelling under the ground, working chiefly by night, a few of these animals, will in a very short time completely mar an otherwise handsome sward. Not only do they make tunnels, the tops of which are likely to fall in with a very slight pressure, but in the course of their travellings they will, at frequent intervals, throw up hills of soil, giving the surface of the lawn an irregular, hummocky contour.

Moles are not seriously troublesome on well rolled lawns. They will always choose a line of least resistance, and a lawn which is kept well rolled presents an entirely too compact mass for Mr. Mole's comfort in travel. If moles are running through a lawn they should be fought by means of mole traps, which are plunged into the runs and usually catch the animals in the night time. Wherever their presence is detected the course of the tunnel should be followed out, and the earth well tramped down. Poisoned bait has sometimes been used with more or less reported success but from the fact that the mole is essentially a carnivorous animal, it is not exactly plain why it should be easily trapped by poisoned grain seeds. The animal does certainly gnaw the roots of plants, but it does this chiefly because they happen to come in his line of travel, and though he may at times, and under special conditions, take to a vegetarian menu, it is not purely the nature of the beast.

F IRY RINGS AND OTHER FUNGI

Very common in lawns made in a woodland country is the peculiar growth of the fairy ring fungus. By the time it attracts attention the area of growth of the fungus has usually assumed the form of a hollow circle, the band in which the fungus is developed varying in width from six to twelve inches. This method of growth never fails to excite interest and has been indeed the basis of much legendary lore of the Old World. Starting from a central spot the mycelium of this fungus spreads evenly outward in all directions, seemingly exhausting the qualities of the soil for itself as it travels, and consequently, as it dies in the centre and is always growing on the outer margin, the mature spore-bearing fruits take the appearance of the characteristic, ever widening circles. The fairy ring fungus is not actually injurious to the grass; indeed the growth of the grass in the immediate neighbourhood of the fungus is usually very markedly vigorous. Dressings of lime will assist in controlling the spread of the fungus, which certainly is disfiguring.

Rarely there occurs over the lawn a peculiar slime fungus which seems to spread over extensive areas of grass in a single night. Actually it is not parasitical on the grass, and only appears during specially wet seasons. Its presence is first recognised by an irregular patch on the lawn, maybe measuring several feet in each direction, in which every blade of grass, every grass stem, everything in fact within its area, becomes covered with small slaty-gray globules about the size of a pin's head, which on being ruptured emit a soot like powder. The appearance of this slime mold usually disconcerts the gardener, but he may rest at ease. It will disappear almost as quickly as it came, and even though it spreads over the greater portion of the lawn it does no actual damage to the grass. The slime mold fungi spread over anything that happens to come in their way, and in travelling over the surface of the ground swarm upon the grass leaves by accident. It might be well, as a precautionary measure, to give a slight spraying with Bordeaux mixture, using it at about one half the standard strength.

Various other fungi may from time to time be found growing among the grass, yet they are not to be considered as pests of the lawn. Wherever they occur they are generally the fruits of neglect or improper lawn conditions. Occasionally, however, the field mushroom will spring up in a very well kept lawn which has been heavily dressed with stable manure gaining its foothold as a consequence of that very treatment. Very few people object to gathering a few luscious mushrooms from their own lawn, and would possibly resent the idea of the mushroom being called a lawn pest. The fairy ring fungus is also a dainty morsel for the epicure, and is the real "champignon" of the French gourmet.

Timothy should never be put into a lawn mixture. It is a coarse grass which makes a stubble like wheat and after the first year will leave ugly holes in the lawn. The seed is gray-green in colour

English rye has the largest of all the lawn grass seeds, and should be used where quick results are wanted. It germinates almost immediately, makes a rapid growth, and dies the first season. It will stand rough usage. In the South it is used for winter effect

SEEDS OF TIMOTHY AND ENGLISH RYE

What is a lawn grass? The purpose of a mixture Adaptations to various soils Kentucky blue grass and its merits Other fundamental grasses How to buy the seed Weights and measures Prices and qualities Grasses to avoid.

THOUGH each of the lawn seed mixtures of the reputable seed stores may be distinct from all the others, yet the differences are those of degree and not kind. In every case the main reliance is the Kentucky blue grass, in a finely recleaned sample, at the rate of four bushels to the acre. The fescues are added to give the quick effect of a turf in the first year, because they make dense tufts of fine low growing leaves; the red top is used for the purpose of securing a stand in places where the soil may be too acid or too sandy for the Kentucky blue grass; the crested dog's tail is a tough grass which makes a low dense growth early and stands hard wear; English rye is added because it germinates very quickly; the wood meadow grass and some others of the fescues are included because they will make a catch in shady places; and clover is frequently included, not because it will serve any special purpose, but merely because some people like to have clover in a lawn.

The ideal lawn grass is one with a creeping, permanent stem and adapted to the greatest variety of soils. Kentucky blue grass fulfils these requirements, but it takes a long time to grow a good turf from it. Whether a lawn should be seeded with Kentucky blue grass alone, or with one of the numerous lawn mixtures, is a much discussed problem. Circumstances should govern the decision. If an immediate result is wanted the mixtures offer distinct advantages, because they contain some quicker germinating grasses; and if the soil is of an uncertain or mixed quality the mixtures again are valuable, because one grass or another out of the lot will surely fit each special soil condition. Kentucky blue grass, though slow in germinating, makes a strong, permanent turf, but it does not attain its proper development until the third year after sowing.

I must confess a prejudice in favour of the mixture if only because I get a quicker result. That alone is worth a great deal in ninety- nine cases out of every hundred. If you can afford to wait two or three years for the lawn to assume a properly green appearance, it may be safe to seed it with one kind of grass.

"But these extra grasses are wasted?" you inquire. I do not think so. It is true that the lawn will eventually become a blue grass lawn, but that will not be until several years after the making, and in the meantime you will have a lawn to enjoy. Moreover the quick growing grasses exclude weeds, and you get a better turf because you get more grass plants to the square foot than if only one grass is sown.

When a large area is to be turned into a lawn, and the preparation of the soil can be carried out practically without regard to the cost, and there is no hurry about results, it may be good to sow only one kind of grass. But in actual practice these ideal conditions rarely, if ever, exist; and particularly on the average small lawn around the suburban home there are various conditions of shade, partial shade, drainage, and soil.

The chances are that the contractor has spread over the former top soil a rich assortment of sundry materials of totally different characters. The proper method of remaking the soil into one of uniform texture and character has been discussed elsewhere, but usually one cannot (or is not willing to) wait a year longer, and there are considerations of expense and appearance also. The trees and shrubs and the buildings will cast shadows on the lawn, giving a mixed effect even when a uniform surface of one grass is presented, and therefore the use of a mixture, giving, of course, more or less uneven expanse of colour, is not objectionable. The different grasses which go to make up a well balanced mixture will blend with each other and even if in certain peculiar situations one grass flourishes more than another does elsewhere on the same lawn, the total result will be pleasing. The essential point about the lawn is that the surface be of one continuous texture. This result will be derived more easily from the use of a mixture of seeds than from one pure grass in the open and another totally different, in the shade, where the other has failed to grow properly. The famous Kentucky blue grass (Poa pratensis is the best single grass to use for a lawn, and it thrives on any but an acid soil. When the Kentucky blue grass will not grow (other things being equal), it is a sign that the soil stands in need of a dressing of lime, which can be applied at the rate of one bushel to a thousand square feet. But when it will grow it will eventually make a good lawn. Unfortunately it does not maintain a fresh green colour in the middle of the summer, and it is comparatively an expensive seed. It is a strong-growing grass, however, and when used in mixtures generally crowds out the other grasses in the course of a few years. Yet, since this grass combines more desirable qualities than any other, it should be used as the chief ingredient for lawns along the Atlantic coast north of Washington and along the Alleghany range as far south as Georgia. It is also used on the Pacific coast. The success of this grass is assured on a limestone formation; but on the coast line and on bottom land there is a likelihood of the soil being acid. In such places one of the species of Agrostis will give better results, as at Newport, R. I., where the Rhode Island bent and red top are extensively used.

It is in order to provide for any such conditions occurring locally as is often the case even in a very small lawn that these grasses enter into lawn mixtures, so that if the blue grass finds the soil uncongenial, yet the ground will not remain bare. Another reason for seeding these grasses is that they germinate quickly and give results the first year. Their foliage is fine and the creeping stems form a dense turf, very effectually binding loose soils.

Rhode Island bent grass also acts as "nurse" to the blue grass when it germinates in the early warm days of the following spring. If a lawn is sown down with pure Kentucky blue grass in the fall there will be no result whatever until the next spring, when, however, it will start earlier than from spring seeding.

If I wanted to secure a greensward for immediate effect, and especially if it were late in the fall season, I would sow freely Pacey's rye (Lolium perenne, var. tenue, a fine-leaved form of English rye grass that is specially adapted to lawns), adding it to any other grasses that may be used (not substituting) at the rate of three pounds to the acre. It is practically an annual grass in this country.

This English rye will start growth almost as soon as sown, and in a month it will make a presentable sheet of green. It is not a permanent grass, however, being a biennial in this country, and will be obliterated by the mowing during the second season.

Rye grass will stand hard usage and permits the free use of the lawn during the first season. It has been successfully used on athletic club grounds (e. g. the baseball diamond, Manhattan Field, New York City) to reseed each year when the "permanent" grasses became worn and it was not possible to leave the lawn untouched for a season. It has not a very fine foliage, and used too freely would result in a coarse looking sward.

FOR SHADED PLACES If there are specially shaded places on the proposed lawn site it will be well to procure a different mixture to be used on these spots. In places of varying degrees of shade it is difficult to estimate the requirments so as to decide whether a pure shade grass shall be used. Therefore, as before, in considering soil conditions, it is the part of wisdom to use a mixture, which includes shade loving grasses. The best of these is the wood meadow grass (Poa nem-oralis, which thrives under trees where other grasses fail. The crested dog's tail (Cynosurus cristatus and the fine-leaved fescue (Festuca ovinay var. tenuifolia) are others to be used. The last named is a "bunch" or "stool" grass, a type that generally speaking should not be admitted to the lawn, but as exceptional situations require exceptional treatment we are justified in including this, the finest leaved and most slender growing of the bunching grasses. Moreover it is a good bottom grass and fills out well near the ground. As a matter of fact the grass in heavily shaded spots is not cut so frequently nor so closely as that in the open which is growing well, and the habit of the fescue is therefore of some advantage.

The crested dog's tail is admirably adapted to mixing with the Kentucky blue grass because its foliage is of the same colour and its habit of growth is similar. Therefore it is usually included in shade mixtures. It is of no moment which one gains a foothold. To the casual observer the lawn presents an uninterrupted sheet of one colour. As a matter of fact the lawn is something to be seen as a whole, from a distance, and a slight variation of leaf in the grasses is of little or no moment. If the site be damp as well as shaded the rough-stalked meadow grass (Poa tfivialts) should be substituted for the fescue. Orchard grass is occasionally included in shade mixtures, but it can be omitted to advantage, for it is a coarse-leaved plant and makes a tuft, not an even sward.

ON SANDY SOIL

As has been indicated, the species of Agros-tis are specially adapted to sandy situations. The Rhode Island bent grass (A. canind and the creeping bent or florin (. alba, var. stoloni-ferd) are the foundation of mixtures for such soils, although unless the land shows an acid reaction it would be well to include some Kentucky blue grass in the mixture, just because if it will make a stand the general appearance of the lawn is improved by just so much. The colour of the bent lacks the richness of the blue grass. The red top (A. alba, var. vulgaris), though adapted to moist clay soil, is often included in mixtures for sandy land because of its ability to make a satisfactory growth upon a slightly acid soil.

OTHER SPECIAL FEATURES

Other grasses are put into mixtures for more or less fancy purposes, and cannot be said to be generally essential. Thus the sweet vernal (Antboxanthum odoratuni) lends fragrance when the lawn is mown.

Every once in a while a statement appears advising that timothy be used in a lawn mixture, as a nurse. As a matter of fact it is a coarse grass which stubbles, and is absolutely unsuited for use on any lawn for ornamental purposes which is regularly mowed. It will die out after the second year, leaving ugly holes that have to be patched over or reseeded with Kentucky blue grass. It may be admitted in wide meadow effects, as it will be crowded out by the creepers and the holes it makes are not eyesores in such situations. It is a general rule that no "bunch" grass should go into a lawn. The only exception being that of the one fescue spoken as admissable in shady places.

SHALL I ADD CLOVER?

Very frequently white clover (Trifolium repens, var. perenne) is added to the lawn-grass seed. Whether or not it shall be used is purely a matter of personal fancy. It does no harm, it keeps green, and it amuses. Some people like to have clover on the lawn; others don't. Just suit yourself, but remember that white clover always enters into the store mixtures, the allowance being about two pounds (one quart) to the acre.

It has this advantage, however: it will make a green covering in places where many of the grass seeds fail entirely, and on certain inert, infertile soils it is not an unusual thing to see a better stand of clover than of the grasses themselves. Indeed, so far as appearance goes, a clover lawn is not at all objectionable. The white clover makes a dense, quickly spreading, low growth and its flat leaves give an even smooth texture to the eye; but it is not a growth that will stand rough usage.

BUYING THE SEED It is especially necessary when buying Kentucky blue grass to pay attention to the various grades in which it is offered. "If you have to shade your price it is easy to shade the quality." This is an axiom which should be remembered by the purchaser, as it applies to grass seed mixtures with special force. Kentucky blue grass is offered in grades varying from 50 per cent, chaff to all pure seed containing no chaff whatever, and as the price is based entirely on the weight of the actual seed contained it is much better to buy by the pound than by the quart. Ask the seedsman for "recleaned fancy" Kentucky blue grass, which may weigh even as high as thirty pounds to the actually measured bushel. In trade usage fourteen pounds of actual seed is regarded as a standard bushel and is sold as a bushel independently of its actual bulk. Thus, of the poorer grades, you may have two bushels of bulk and get one bushel of seed.

A mixture of high grade thoroughly re-cleaned fancy seed would vary in price from 4.50 to 5 per bushel according to the quantities of the rarer or special grasses that were included in the mixture, and cannot be sold very much cheaper even in bulk. Cheaper mixtures can be bought, and I have seen excellent results the first year from lawns which have been seeded with mixtures that cost as low as 3 per bushel. Indeed, further than this, one gentleman once pointed out to me with great pride a lawn of about five acres in extent, on which he had used two mixtures, one costing 5 a bushel, the other 3 a bushel.

He was rejoicing immensely over the fact that he had succeeded in producing a better looking lawn with the lower priced seed than he had with the more expensive one. That was his opinion the first year after sowing. The uninitiated will he easily misled by these appearances. The cheaper mixture, assuming of course, that in each case thoroughly recleaned seed was used, gives the better earlier result because it has a larger percentage of quick growing grasses which will eventually run out. In the higher priced mixture where ultimate effect is sought rather than early effect, the more permanent grasses make a slower start, but the results are eminently more satisfactory in the third year.

WHAT TO AVOID

For lawn making any and all grasses that form tufts, or stools or bunches, as they are sometimes called; and grasses which do not spread continuously by creeping stems; or that have too tall a growth without an abundance of bottom leaves; or that die out after a year or two's occupancy of the ground, are utterly unreliable. Samples of these are the well-known orchard grass, timothy, tall meadow fescue, hard fescue, and the oat grasses. In northern climates the Bermuda grass is not desirable because of its rusty brown appearance as soon as the cold weather touches it.

FROM the statements made in the foregoing chapter it will be seen that no one grass, nor one combination of several grasses, is equally adapted for all soils and all situations. It is doubtful indeed whether one mixture can be given for exact results; on the same sort of soil in different situations but practically these minute differences need not cause any concern. The object throughout the Eastern States is to establish the Kentucky blue grass wherever it will succeed; and the prime reason for adding other grasses is to cover the ground before the Kentucky blue grass has become established, and therefore to occupy the ground to the exclusion of weeds. There is, however, another very essential service rendered by these extra grasses: the fact that the Kentucky blue grass does not carpet the ground as closely and as low down as some of the others makes it desirable to employ one of them to give a green appearance to the lawn immediately after cutting. Yet another point is this: that mixtures result in a denser turf at an early date because curiously enough more grasses will grow to a given area if there is a mixture of various species than would be the case were one grass alone used.

A PRACTICAL FORMULA

A thoroughly practical formula that has been tried on soils of average fertility and composition, and which has given thorough satisfaction is as follows:

Kentucky blue 10 quarts

Rhode Island bent 8 quarts

English rye 3 quarts

This is a crude, although reliable mixture. Indeed it may be called a lawn mixture reduced to its simplest elements. The quantities given in quarts are based on thoroughly recleaned seed.

A more refined mixture, including a fancy red top for filling in during the early years of the lawn and after the English rye has lived its life, is as follows:

Fancy Kentucky blue grass 10 Ibs.

Fancy red top 4 Ibs.

R. I. bent 3 Ibs.

English rye 3 Ibs.

Red top is a variety of bent grass unsurpassed for growing on sandy soils and is the foundation for the lawns at Newport. The seed is much smaller than that of Kentucky blue grass and is about the same size as timothy, but is not so wide, and is easily distinguished by its colour. Red top seed is a light brown; timothy seed is gray-green

The lawn grass mixture should be nearly all of this grass Kentucky blue. It is a permanent grass which takes three years to make a perfect turf, and will in time crowd out any other grasses that are in the mixture if the lawn is made on a rich moist loam, not acid

SEEDS OF THE TWO GOOD LAWN GRASSES

A FIRST-CLASS LAWN MIXTURE

The "lawn mixtures" of the different seed stores differ but little from one another. They are chiefly Kentucky blue grass with rea top, Rhode Island bent, a little English rye, and a small addition of white clover (the round seed shown in the photograph). Frequently crested dog's tail is included. Twenty pounds is a standard weight for a bushel of such a mixture, which is composed of fancy, recleaned seed. Uncleaned seed weighs less to the bushel because of the chaff

This is expressed in weight and may be used as a fair basis of comparison with the preceding formula which is expressed in bulk. This mixture would give twenty pounds to the bushel, and would be sufficient for one fifth of an acre, say about 8,000 square feet. Fancy seed is specified in the formula both as regards the blue grass and the red top. The twenty pounds weight of this mixture, though designated by many dealers as a bushel, would not fill the actual measured bushel.

ADAPTING TO PECULIAR CONDITIONS

This formula can be adapted to special purposes by substituting any one of the special grasses, according to the particular requirements, for equal weight of blue grass. Thusthe wood meadow grass could be used in the proportion of two to three pounds where it became necessary to seed a space that was shaded by trees, Kentucky blue grass being reduced to 7 pounds. By referring to the table on page 162 a list of substitute grasses will be seen, and notes are given as to their special characteristics and purposes. The following are approved formulas:

Mixture for Shaded Places

Kentucky blue grass 40 per cent.

Wood meadow grass 40 ""

Various leaved fescue. 10 ""

Crested dog's tail 10 ""

Mixture for Terrace and Slopes

Creeping bent (or Rhode Island bent) 40 per cent.

Crested dog's tail 25 ""

Canada blue grass 25 ""

Kentucky blue grass 10 ""

The purpose here is to secure quick growing, deep rooting grasses that will bind the soil until such time as the permanent grasses are in possession.   Also some consideration should be given to the fact that such situations may be either extremely dry or at times abnormally wet.

Mixture for Putting Green

Crested dog's tail 30 per cent.

Creeping bent 35 ""

Rhode Island bent 35 ""

The essential quality here is a mixture of grasses that will give a dense short turf which can be kept closely cropped and will stand a great deal of trampling. For this reason the blue grass and clover are inadmissible.

SEED MIXTURES FOR SPECIAL PURPOSES 105 Mixture for the Fair Green

Red top 35 per cent.

Kentucky blue grass 35 ""

Meadow fescue 10 ""

English rye 20 ""

Much coarser growing grasses can be admitted here than are desirable for the putting green. The grass will not be cut so frequently and there is no objection to a certain amount of coarse vigorous growth. Cheaper grasses can be used in quantity.

Mixture for Sandy Soils

Kentucky blue grass 25 per cent.

Creeping bent 30 ""

Rhode Island bent 30 ""

Fine leaved fescue 15 ""

Sandy soils are usually dry without much bottom, and to establish a lawn requires quickly growing binding grasses which will withstand drought. If the sand is acid Kentucky blue grass cannot be counted upon to succeed unless that condition can be corrected by dressings of lime.

Mixture for Seaside Lawns
Rhode Island bent 30 per cent.
Creeping bent 30 ""
Kentucky blue grass 25 ""

Usually there is considerable difficulty in establishing Kentucky blue grass in maritime regions. There is a good field for progressive work in introducing suitable grasses for lawns on the sea coast. At the present time the chief reliance is on some of the species of Agrostis or bent grasses. This mixture should result in a substantial lawn on any sort of soil. The beach grass wih take a hold where the blue grass fails, but it is, generally, not a desirable lawn grass.

Mixture for Clay Soils
Kentucky blue grass 50 per cent.
English rye 20 ""
Fancy red top 30 ""

Generally with very little preparation, so as to improve the physical condition and drainage, these soils will maintain excellent blue grass lawns. The rye grass recommended gives the early quick result, the red top makes a bottom grass, and the blue grass is the permanent feature.

Mixture for Wet and Bottom Lands
Kentucky blue grass 30 per cent.
Rough stalk meadow grass 30 ""
English rye 20 ""
Various leaved fescue. 20 ""

There are various grades of red top offered weighing from fourteen to thirty-six pounds to the measured bushel. Fancy red top seed will range from thirty to thirty-five pounds per bushel and has no chaff.

Of course grasses that are particularly adapted to sandy soils must be omitted here. Fortunately Kentucky blue grass will thrive on moist soils, and should form a very large percentage of the mixture. In order to keep out the weeds a fair percentage of the quickly growing rye grass is included. The rough stalk meadow grass is essentially a wet land grass and will thrive nowhere else.

Mixture for Hill Tops
Kentucky blue grass 40 per cent.
Rhode Island bent 25 ""
Creeping bent 20 ""
Sheep fescue 10 ""
White clover 05 ""

To a certain extent the same grasses as are recommended for terrace mixture may be used on hill tops, provided the situation has a good soil and does not become unduly dry. Rapidly creeping, binding grasses are essential, and white clover should never be omitted because it will make a quick growth and carpet the ground in places where the grasses fail to make a stand.

SPECIAL NOTES OF INTEREST

These formulas are expressed in percentages by weight in order that the reader may gain some graphic idea of the relationships of the various grasses.

It is assumed that thoroughly recleaned fancy grades may be used throughout. There is no use whatever buying the lower grade samples which may consist of fifty per cent, chaff.

Clover is not included in all the foregoing formulas but may be added if fancy dictates, and it had better be sown separately, after the grass seeds, because, being a heavy seed, it is likely to settle to the bottom of the mixture.

These formulas are in every case merely suggestive and in practice can possibly be modified in every case to the great advantage of all concerned. There is no such thing as a universally best mixture. A comparison of the foregoing formulas with the following table and the exercise of common sense will yield more satisfactory results than the strict adherence to the printed text.

The difficulties of southern climates Heat resistant grasses and substitutes A hardy Bermuda grass Perfect lawns for the South, California and Arizona.

IN THE Southern States, and where subtropical conditions prevail, the problem of lawn making differs from that which is met in the Northern States. In the latter region the Kentucky blue grass is the basis of all good lawns, and indeed there is no better grass for making a permanent green sward. But, unfortunately, while it is adapted to a very great variety of soils and situations, it cannot stand the excessive heat of the Southern summers. South of the latitude of Washington D. C., except in the Alleghany Range, where the blue grass will grow as far south as north- ern Georgia, some substitute for Kentucky blue grass must be sought. On the lighter soils white clover, red top, and Rhode Island bent are more to be relied upon, and they make a beautiful soft lawn, but they lack the permanent character of the Kentucky blue grass.

South of Washington white clover forms an important feature of all lawns and as the subtropical regions are approached, the grass gradually gives place to the clover. As one proceeds south, and as the region of the Kentucky grass ends, the region of Bermuda grass (Capriola, or Cynodon t Dactylon) begins. This may be regarded as the permanent lawn grass of the South. It is a rapidly creeping grass, makes a substantial growth in warm weather, but unfortunately suffers from cold and turns brown as soon as frost touches it. Though the roots are permanent and will survive the winters the top dies, and in the northern regions of the southern section of the country, some substitute or rather companion grass is necessary to give the green appearance during winter. It is particularly adapted to the sandy soils of the Atlantic coast plain, standing heat and drought, and it may be mown over frequently.

A system of double seeding is resorted to where Bermuda grass lawns suffer from frost in the winter. In order to keep the green colour all the year around, English rye grass is annually scattered over the lawn at the rate of about fifty pounds to the acre. This is done about the end of September or the beginning of October, first raking over the surface of the soil and applying a top dressing from the compost heap. This seed will germinate in a week, and by the middle of November will have formed a perfect lawn, which will remain green all the winter. By the following May it will have died, just at the time when the Bermuda grass is again starting into growth. It has been found that ploughing in from seven hundred and fifty to a thousand pounds of cotton seed meal to the acre before sowing or planting the Bermuda grass (which work is done in January at the rate of six pounds to the acre) puts the soil in excellent condition. Surface dressings of cotton seed meal may also be given after scarifying in the fall, previous to broadcasting the rye seed.

A HARDIER BERMUDA GRASS

There is a specially hardy form of the Bermuda grass which has been introduced into Oklahoma within the last few years, and seems to be well adapted to that latitude, although it may be of doubtful value in the northern parts of the state. This grass, after fourteen years of experiment and observation, has been proved to be better adapted for lawn purposes in this state than is the commoner form which freezes black in winter and remains as a disfigurement on the ground until late May. The hardy form begins its growth during the last days of March. As an illustration of its suitability it may be stated that on the College Campus, at Stillwater, where Kentucky blue grass failed as did all kinds of mixtures, including the fescues and the clovers this hardy Bermuda grass formed a complete lawn in three seasons. It remains green from April to October.

Bermuda grass is generally propagated by cuttings or rather, to be more correct, by small pieces of turf which are planted a few inches apart and will eventually grow together to form a perfect turf.

ST. AUGUSTINE GRASS FOR FLORIDA

Still farther south, in Florida, where still different conditions prevail a much warmer climate and greater humidity there is opportunity for yet other grasses to be used for lawns, and the St. Augustine grass (Steno-tapbrum secundatum also known as S. Amen-canum) is the grass relied upon for lawn purposes. It has a coarse and very upright leaf but a creeping root stock. It remains in a green condition practically throughout the whole year, and, so far as giving the green colour so desirable for landscape effects is concerned, answers every requirement. It is not, however, a perfect lawn grass. It is adapted to a wide area and succeeds in the West Indies displacing the Bermuda grass even in the Island of Bermuda.

THE KOREAN LAWN GRASS

From Charlestown, south along the sea-coast, very satisfactory results have been obtained by the use of the Korean lawn grass known to botanists by the name of Osterdarma matrella. This is a creeping or stoloniferous grass with rather rigid often sharp pointed leaves and tapering tender spikelets. Two or three other species of the genus have been introduced but the one named is reported upon by Professor L. C. Corbett (Farmers' Bulletin No. 248) in these words: "It thrives well in the latitude of Washington, but the leaves are not hardy and assume a straw colour in winter. It will, however, undoubtedly be a decided acquisition for lawns near the seashore in latitudes south of Washington."

In the Gulf Coast country, what is known as carpet grass (Paspalum compressurri) has been receiving extended favour and appears to be a very suitable companion to the Bermuda grass. It is readily propagated in the same way as the latter, but it also seeds.

This is one of the best pasture grasses of the low moist country along the Gulf Coast, and it is here that it may be expected to find its chief use as a lawn grass, although its range of distribution is from Virginia to Texas. In the dryer regions of our western prairies the Buffalo grass (Bulbilis dactyloides) is becoming established.

HOW SOUTHERN CALIFORNIA GOT ITS LAWN PLANTS

But perhaps the most promising of all the lawn grass substitutes for southern and dry regions is the fog plant (Lippia nodi flora.

Dr. F. Franceschi of Santa Barbara has given most favourable reports on its behaviour in southern California, lawns having been successfully established where otherwise no sort of success has been achieved.

Dr. Franceschi gives this account of its introduction:

"It was in 1869, barely one year before the fall of the second Empire, when the centennial of the first Napoleon was celebrated with great festivities at his birthplace, Ajaccio, in Corsica. The Superintendent of Parks of the City of Florence, Signor Pucci, to whom the floral decorations had been entrusted, was quite struck with Lippia, as it had been used in the public garden of Ajaccio. He took some with him to Florence, and put it on trial in one of the public gardens. There it did so well that it soon spread to other parts of Italy, and particularly along the Riviera, where the climatic conditions are very much like southern California.

"In the year 1898 my daughter who had recently come from Italy, called my attention to the fact that for several years already Lippia had been used to carpet the esplanade at the Naval Academy at Leghorn, where 500 boys had their daily drilling, and all sorts of games. It was obvious to think that if Lippia had done so well in Italy it ought to do the same in California. From the Director of the Botanic Garden in Rome I secured by mail a small tin box of Lippia plants (less than 12 ounces weight). Now, after six years, there are hundreds and hundreds of acres planted with Lippia, between California, Arizona, Mexico, and Australia, and it all came out of that small tin box. And had it not been for the celebration of the centennial of the great Napoleon, probably this humble plant would still grow, little known and unappreciated, only on the coast of Corsica and other points along the Mediterranean."

The following are the cultural directions for establishing lawns of this plant:

Have your ground well worked and pulverised, levelled, and rolled if possible. No manure recommended.

Lippia seeds very sparingly or not at all. Anyhow, the best and quickest way to propagate it is by planting small sods (two square inches) at a distance of about one, or two, or more feet apart. The closer it is planted the sooner the ground will be carpeted. Each small sod contains many joints, and from each joint runners and roots will soon appear that will branch in every direction, and will anchor it in the ground, rooting again as they run.

Press and well firm the sods in the ground and give sufficient water to start growth. Occasional rolling will be of advantage. Frequent walking over it will have the same effect.

If the tiny lilac flowers (much sought after by the bees) are not desired, they can easily be removed by an ordinary lawn mower.

During the dry season water must be given with a lawn sprinkler or otherwise, at intervals as the local conditions will suggest.

Much experimental research is now being carried on by the Department of Agriculture, with a view to discovering some substitute grass which will be for the South what the Kentucky blue grass is for the North. Among subjects of recent investigation are various species of clover and grasses imported from Asia and Australia. It is unfortunately too early at this time to state definite results concerning these imported lawn substitutes, but attention is called to them so that the inquiring reader may follow up the lines of investigation.

The few essentials Types of mowers The power mower Preventing damage from horses Rollers Sweepers Rakes Weeders Trimming tools The use of the shears The simple grass hook Hose, and hose Keeping life in it Turfing irons The scythe.

THE essential tools for making and maintaining a lawn are comparatively few. The possible tools are many. At the beginning of things a good plough, a sub-soil plough, and a steel-toothed harrow must be had, but these can hardly be properly called lawn tools; they are equally essential to the fundamental ground work of any part of the estate. The special tools for after maintenance consist of the lawn mower, the roller, and the rake.

FOR CUTTING

The mower can be had in various patterns and at prices ranging upward from two and a half dollars, the figure varying both with the style of construction and the width of the cut.

BEST LAWN TOOLS AND THEIR USE Iig

For all ordinary purposes buy a lawn mower not less than twelve inches wide. If the lawn is of any size above that common in the ordinary suburban lot it will be wise economy to procure a machine of not less than sixteen-inch cut, and where the labour can be easily had, it may be well to go several sizes larger even up to twenty-one inches.

At the best of times, and under the best of conditions, the work of mowing the lawn is somewhat burdensome, therefore buy a mower of the ball bearing type. The ease with which a machine of this type can be operated as compared with one of the older articles, is something extraordinary. A mere child can very well handle a medium sized machine of the modern light running model. There is absolutely no reason why you should make yourself a draught-horse when the inconvenience can be avoided for many years by the investment of a five dollar bill in the beginning. All modern lawn mowers throw the clippings to the rear so that they may be left on the lawn when the machine is used without a catch-box, as is usually the case where mowing is done at frequent intervals.

For large lawns mowers drawn by horses are great time savers, and if a horse is kept at all the purchase of a horse mower should be decided on at once. It takes very little time to hitch up the horse of an evening and run over the lawn. For the average garden there is no neccessity to buy a mower which can be set very close to the ground; in fact, the possibility of being able to shave the surface is a dangerous feature, in the majority of cases.

For putting greens, where as low clean-cut and even a surface as possibleis essential, a special type of mower is used, and it can be taken over the ground after the cutting with a machine of the regular type. In general a lawn should not be cut closer than two inches.

Some mowers combine rollers with the knives. These are most useful on narrow strips of grass bordering walks or flower beds where it is impossible to use the heavier type of roller. But the light weight of the machine that is involved with ease of manipulation, for the average purpose, renders the roller useless as a factor in the maintenance of the lawn. It is only in the larger type of machine, which is drawn by a horse and which carries the driver upon it, that the rollers be-

THE PROPER KIND OF ROLLER

Persistent rolling is of vital importance in the maintenance of a lawn. Use a sectional roller because turns can be made without injuring the grass, the sections working independently. The water ballast roller can be weighted to suit the strength of the operator, varying from three to six hundred pounds come efficient, therefore it is far better to separate the two tools and have the small rollers on the mower merely for the purpose of supporting the rest of the machine. Large driving wheels are an advantage. They give a high gearing and the knives being operated at a high speed cut more evenly and with less pull. When properly adjusted the knives sharpen themselves on the plate, the only care necessary being to keep the machine clean.

For very large estates the motor combined lawn mower and roller is an engine that should be considered. The thorough and frequent rolling that a lawn will thus receive is a factor of considerable importance in favour of such a machine. They will weigh up to three thousand pounds, and the two operations of rolling and cutting can be conducted at one time without the use of a horse. Such great pressure effectually stamps out crab grass.

There is always this drawback to the use of a horse on the lawn: that holes will be made by the feet. This is obviated to some extent by the use of lawn horse shoes, contrivances of leather and wood which are tied over the hoofs, thus distributing the weight over a larger area. It is unfortunately true that the greater necessity for rolling exists at the time of year when the ground is most susceptible to surface injuries.

WEIGHT OF ROLLER

The roller should weigh three hundred pounds, or even more if there is a man strong enough to operate one of greater weight. Heavy rolling in the spring saves the lawn from burning in the summer and obviates, in a degree that is very rarely understood, the necessity for summer watering. Therefore the heavier the roller the better. One man should be able to operate a three hundred pound roller, but it will take two people to properly use a heavier tool.

Lawn rollers are also made with weight boxes attached by which the weight of the tool can be adjusted to the strength of the operator. It is no use buying a roller which weighs less than two hundred and fifty pounds. Of the larger size draught rollers there are many patterns and they can be had in all weights up to two thousand pounds, which will cover a track of six feet. The smaller-sized rollers which are adapted for general use will cover a track of twenty inches.

An ingenious improvement is the water ballast roller in which the cylinder is ballasted with water or sand so as to increase its weight by which means a three hundred pound machine can have its efficiency actually doubled.

It is important to buy a sectional roller for lawns. The smaller sizes are made in two sections and the larger horse-power rollers will run up to six sections. The great advantage of this arrangement is in the ease with which the tool can be turned without tearing or dragging the surface of the lawn.

For cleaning up grass clippings or fallen leaves, sweeping machines are made but generally the work is done by hand rakes. These are of light construction, very wide, and are either wood or steel wire made in a series or arched teeth. For scarifying the surface of the lawn, as for instance when it is necessary to haul up crab grass or for seeding, an ordinary sharp-pronged steel garden rake is much better.

For deep-rooted weeds like dandelion there are a number of special weeders which are attached to long handles and which enable the operator to work without getting down on his hands and knees.

These tools all operate on the principle of cutting off the crown of the plant an inch or two below the surface and some of them have a claw, or other gathering arrangement, by which the severed crown can be lifted and thrown into a handy receptacle. Others again are made on the style of a gouge by which a cylinder of soil containing the root is withdrawn.

A very simple and the most handy tool of its kind for use where the worker does not object to bending his back or getting down on his knees is what is known as the American asparagus knife. Though introduced primarily for plunging into the asparagus beds to cut off the young growth some inches below the ground, it has been found to be especially adapted as a lawn weeder and is more often used for this adventitious purpose than it is for the purpose for which it was especially designed! This consists of a steel blade about ten or twelve inches long, widest at the top where it has an expanse of about an inch and a half. A V-shaped notch at this end which is rough sharpened with a chisel edge can be thrust deeply into the ground for cutting off such roots as dandelion or dock or it may be used as a surface shaver in attacking plantains. All these small weeding appliances range in price from twenty-five cents to half a dollar, and earn their money's worth easily in the first season.

When cutting out large strong growing weeds with long roots, holes are made in the lawn which must be filled with good garden soil and immediately sprinkled over with a pinch of lawn mixture, so that the grass may take immediate hold to the entire exclusion of weeds.

EDGING AND TRIMMING TOOLS

The edge of the lawn where it borders walks or flower beds needs careful trimming and maintenance. If it becomes irregular or is battered down, very much of the neat appearance of the lawn itself is lost. The traffic across the lawn will also have a tendency to batter down the edges. Once a week, when mowing is taken in hand, the edges should be carefully examined, and with the garden rake, turned upside down, any broken portions may be easily rebuilt. If this little detail is attended to regularly, and the damage not allowed to become exaggerated, it is surprising how little time and work will be occupied in maintaining a decent appearance.

The lawn mower will not cut the edges, and although there are attachments made for certain styles of mowers and even special edge cutters in machine form, it cannot be said that they have proved practically successful. They easily become clogged with dirt or pick up stones and the cutting edge is damaged. Then the irregularity of the height of the lawn above its surroundings renders it somewhat difficult to exactly gauge the depth to which such a cutter should be set. In actual practice, even on the very largest estates, it is found better to use what is known as edging shears for trimming. The man handling the shears usually follows the man with the mower. These shears, which are set in long handles, the knives working upward and downward, can be used very easily and any irregularity or unevenness of the surface or the edge itself is easily followed and the grass trimmed off accurately.

Even in small gardens it is worth while to invest in a pair of edging shears rather than the spring shears sometimes referred to as sheep shears, which are frequently used by suburbanites, not only for trimming, but even for cutting the entire surface. Work with this tool is laborious, and, except for trimming, will result in an irregular patchy job.

The sheep shears should, however, form part of the equipment of the lawn tool outfit. They are really necessary for finishing off in angles of buildings or the borders of formal beds, and especially for trimming after the mower close up to the trunks of trees or masses of shrubbery where it is not possible to run the machine. Particular care should be exercised to keep the lawn mower well clear of the bases of trees or overhanging branches of shrubberies which skirt the lawn. In the one case there is danger of "barking" the trees from the projecting parts of the mower, and it is utterly impossible to run the knives directly up to the tree; in the other case the mower is likely to clip off a lower growth of the shrubs just where they form unions-with the grass. This will result in giving the shrubbery itself an appearance of being an excrescence upon the lawn a thing set down upon it accidentally and improperly, rather than part of a happy and tasteful composition and union in the surrounding borders and distant masses of other shrubs and trees. After the mower has been used to cut the larger surface of the grass the spring shears are taken in hand and any untouched corners or tufts of grass are hand trimmed.

Another useful hand cutter is the grass hook, a modified form of sickle designed especially for cutting grass with a sharp, easy swing. It is a sort of miniature scythe. Its disadvantage is that one has to crawl over the ground when working. It is useful in small gardens, however, where there are narrow borders of grass, for which it would hardly be worth while purchasing a machine mower with small knives.

The edging iron, which is used for trimming the edges, is a serviceable tool but is hardly a necessary part of the equipment for the amateur with only a city lot. This tool consists of a half circle of steel set in a handle, and is used to trim around borders and curves. It is specially serviceable for straightening up and squaring sides of the lawn which have spread over their original line. This trueing becomes necessary every once in a while, because the traffic and the natural inclination of the soil to spread and level out uneven edges tends to destroy the strict original line.

In the spring time it is well indeed to take the garden line and, by means of it and a two-edged board, follow around all the edges of the lawn with the edging iron, cutting down into the ground below and thus straightening out the unevennesses that may have resulted from the winter.

THE HOSE AND ITS CARE

Notwithstanding what has been previously said regarding the use of the hose and the propriety of watering as little as practicable, a hose should enter into the equipment. The standard rubber hose is known as four ply, and perhaps more particularly in the hose than in any other of the tools it is economy to buy the highest-priced goods on the market. Cheap hose is the most costly in the long run. A good quality pure rubber hose will last several seasons whereas the cheaper article will generally be worn out before it has been used twelve months. Exposure to the air, and the fact of being continually wet, is destructive to any but the very best quality of rubber, and further the water pressure is a matter of much moment. If a high-pressure city supply is used for watering the garden it will often be necessary to have a hose that will stand pressure up to two hundred pounds. Many of the poorer grades of hose offered are not guaranteed above seventy-five pounds. The difference in price of the two qualities is about 30 per cent. Unless the ground is peculiarly rocky a plain hose is better than an armoured hose. This latter consists of a rubber hose which is wound over by a spiral wire covering. It is considerably heavier in use, but its worst characteristic is that when dragged across a lawn, and especially on edges crossing walks, it cuts into the surface and makes ugly channels, particularly if the ground is wet and loose.

Garden hose is regularly manufactured in multiples of twenty-five feet lengths. There is a great advantage in having just a little more than is actually necessary. The reserve length is always handy in case of accident and the consequent necessity of cutting down one of the sections. As offered in the stores the hose comes conplete with front and end couplings for attachment to the faucet and for uniting with any other length. The standard dimensions of garden hose are three quarter inch and one inch hose. It is better to use the larger size.

Nozzles to be used on the hose are of various types. One of the best is what is known as the graduating spray. By means of this attachment the water can be thrown in a fine or coarse spray or in a solid jet. This adds considerably to the general utility of the hose and it can be used as well for watering and for washing.

After use the hose should be carefully wound up and taken inside, out of the sun. Never leave it lying around when out of use, and never allow it to stand loaded with water.

The stop nozzle, though occasionally convenient, is often dangerous. Far better to throw the end of the hose down on the lawn letting the water run from it, then run back to the stand pipe or faucet, cutting off the supply at that point.

If you have more than twenty-five feet of hose some arrangement for winding it is a great convenience. The hose reel is usually made with travel wheels; the union being made with the stand pipe the reel can be wheeled out into the garden thus extending the hose in the direction in which it is to be used. If the hose is wound on to the reel after use it will be practically drained of water, and the gathering up is done without any dragging over the surface and cutting the edges of the lawn, or scratching the hose itself by being drawn over gravel walks.

In lawn making from sods the turfing iron is indispensable. This consists essentially of a long necked thin flat spade fitted at such an angle that it works flat on the ground, or rather in the ground, as it is used under the sod both for cutting and relaying. Its use in laying or repairing with sods lies in the ease with which, by its means, any ir-regularites of the surface or of the sod can be straightened out. For instance, if a sod of uneven depth is laid down it is easy with the turfing iron either to cut out the ground from below at one end or to distribute properly the quantity of loose soil at the other end soil which is always kept handy in the wheelbarrow when working on the lawn, and from which a handful is taken and thrown under the sod.

THE NEGLECTED SCYTHE

Just because so few people nowadays understand its manipulation, the scythe the ideal cutting instrument has fallen into disuse. For newly made lawns it is infinitely superior to the lawn mower as it cuts without tearing, without pulling. And a lawn mowed by an expert shows no signs whatever of having been cut. The inevitable streakiness which follows the use of the lawn mower operated in different directions is not seen after the scythe is used. Another advantage of this instrument is that the depth at which it will cut can be graded to a nicety, and there is no necessity to follow it up with trimming shears because it can be used in the sharpest corners. Its use is restricted, however, to very large lawns and it is not a tool to which the amateur gardener need give any attention.

Solid marginal planting of evergreens and deciduous shrubbery bordering the public road, thus securing absolute privacy. (View on a Lenox estate)

The bed of lily-of-the-valley successfully solves the problem of what to plant under the trees and it also gives a reason for the curve in the walk

LAWN PICTURES I

CHAPTER XII How To MAKE LAWN PICTURES

The artistic qualities of the lawn Grouping trees and shrubs Two main styles of treatment Making the most of small areas Colour values Grass walks Locating flower beds Staking the outlines Shaping the beds Making an ellipse Tracing curves and contra curves Art in design Walks Isolated clumps of shrubbery.

CLOSELY associated with the making of the lawn is the planting around it. So close indeed is this association that the term "lawn" has become significant of the general outlook of the grass and shrubbery effect. The greensward is as the canvas on which the artist paints, with living trees and shrubs as his pigments. After all the grass itself is not the picture but only the setting.

OPEN AND BELT PLANTINGS

There are two broad general principles into which all treatments of the marginal planting and surrounding grounds may be grouped. On the one hand is what may be called the open treatment, and on the other the close or belt treatment.

The open treatment is best adapted to large areas where park-like effect is sought. It adds enormously to the apparent distance, and in the hands of a skilful landscape gardener will result in the creation of the most charming compositions and realisations of distant effects. All the beauties of the surrounding landscape may thus be drawn into and made, part of the home grounds. The distant lake, the far off hillside, and the rolling masses of upland and dale, should not be lost by excessive belt planting. Judicious treatment in this style leads the observer's eye, in successive steps from point to point, until he unconsciously connects the whole of the distant landscape with the immediate foreground, and actually deceives himself into a belief of a wide expanse of the property. This is the highest type of landscape composition, one which is all too little thought of by the majority of owners, who fail to draw into their home pictures the salient features of the natural surroundings.

If there is a naturally dense plantingor woodland which cuts off the distant scene it should by all means be opened up. "Vistas" should be made. Everything in the outlying country that is beautiful should be brought into sight of the home lawn; and all mass plantings should be designed with the object of either helping the general composition toward these outlying points, or for the purpose of obliterating whatsoever is ugly and objectionable. This open treatment is not impossible, sometimes, on even very small lawns. It is worth while giving long and earnest thought to the possibilities of the surroundings, and making the plantations of the home garden in direct relation to these other features.

THE SECLUDED GARDEN In crowded, suburban districts, where the distant landscape is merely an accumulation of more or less unpicturesque habitations of man in the conventional form, the happier result is usually had by so massing the plantings around the lawn as to cut off whatever abuts, and so to actually emphasise the seclusion of the home. Primarily the garden is, or should be, a private outdoor room, and the immediate adjoinment of the house ought to be designed in reference to, and in relation with the main lines of the building it supports, rather than with the far distance. These two essentially different yet not inharmonious points of view are too often confused. The results are incongruous or ludicrous. Fancy putting a "cut-off" plantation at the far end of a stretch of a five-acre lawn which comes to look like a mere hedge in the distance, clearly marking a boundary and a separation from the distant view, and having no apparent reason that is no artistic reason for its existence. As in structural art, in architecture, etc., every line and every curve should be a part of the structural scheme, and have its existence justified so also it is with the landscape. Every mass or group of trees should justify itself, or form part of the general whole.

LANDSCAPE IN THE CITY LOT

Open treatment of a small lawn, such as is met with in a city or suburban lot, usually is unsatisfactory because it brings into the lines of sight the more undesirable and obtrusive features of the surrounding lots. But even with the close border planting it is not by any means impossible to increase the apparent distances by means of judicious curves and graceful lines.

Very much may be accomplished in this respect by the use of proper plants which by means of their colour values help in the composition of the picture. Thus, for instance, the white birch planted nearly at the end of a long and narrow stretch of lawn running between shrubbery borders, will, by immediately fixing the eye, create the impression of a much greater depth than actually exists, and especially if beyond this again some few feet away is a mass of planting in which the blue tone is dominant. Yellow colours should be placed only in foregrounds because of the fore-shortening effect that they give us. Masses of yellow foliage or flowers placed at the distant point of the lawn, no matter how skilfully the general plan may have been made, will inevitably result in destroying all sense of perspective.

GRASS WALKS

The grass walk, or turf walk as it is more commonly called, is an all too rarely seen feature of our gardens. In many places where there are parallel borders, separated by only a few feet, the greatest artistic effect, the more reposeful feeling, and certainly the most natural setting and environment for the plants of the border will be made by filling in the intervening space with grass rather than with gravel. These grass walks are something more than extensions of the lawn idea. They unite the different masses of plantings and bring them in as integral parts of the garden itself. Abrupt changes from one style of garden to another should be avoided if possible.

MAKING FLOWER BEDS

Where flower beds are to be placed on the lawn it is far better to treat the whole surface in the first place as one unbroken grass area, cutting in the beds later, when the grass has become thoroughly established. The final result is better because the cut edges will be more sharply defined, and it is far easier, in the first place, to make an unbroken stretch of lawn than it is to work in and out between and around more or less complicated bed outlines.

It is a very easy matter to cut these beds, and, moreover, their form and proportions can be determined in exact relation to each other and to the surroundings.

In starting to make beds on an already established lawn they should be outlined by stout wooden stakes, driven into the ground. These can be adjusted and moved until the area to be converted suits the eye. Use stout wooden stakes about twelve inches long, sharpened at one end, and preferably un-painted. When the stakes have been driven into position a cord can be drawn all around them, which will mark the outline of the future bed. Another advantage from working in this way is that the grass can be taken up in the form of turf and used to patch up any irregularities that have occurred in other parts of the lawn.

The form and outline having been determined, the line can be cut around by plunging a sharp spade into it and working it forward toward the inside of the bed at each thrust. Digging should then commence at the centre of the bed; the work gradually extending outward in a series of circles until the whole of the surface has been turned under. If this is properly done the contour of the bed will be almost perfect and can be easily finished off by means of the garden rake. Of course it would be well to spread manure over the grass before it is dug under.

The edges of the bed should be protected by flat boards which will take the tread of the workmen, and also keep the grass clean. The grass that is turned under should be buried, if possible a foot below the surface, where it will soon rot and add to the humus of the soil. There need be no fear that the grass will grow and make a weedy bed.

HOW TO SHAPE THE BEDS

Beds of regular form can easily be marked out by means of a stake and line. Thus, to make a circular bed, drive a stake in the centre, and with a noosed cord the noose being slipped over the stake, and the cord of a length equal to half the diameter of the desired bed the outline can be scratched on the grass. Use another sharply pointed stake or an iron rod for scratching this outline, and cut the outline deeper by means of an edging iron or spade.

The staking of a square bed is simplicity itself. All that is necessary being four stakes and two true edged boards with which right angles can be marked. In this case begin from one corner driving the stake until it is standing squarely in the ground, then lay one of the boards alongside it, and, measuring off the required distance for the side of the bed, drive another stake. Without removing the first board lay the other one against it at right angles, outside of the stake, and proceed in the same manner until the four sides are marked.

Except in public places, in close proximity to buildings, and even often in such situations also, the ellipse will give a much more satisfactory bed than the true circle, and it can be made just as easily. Here is the method: If only the major axis be known, mark that on the

AB is the major axis of the ellipse. Divide this line into three equal parts, at D and C. With D as centre and distance DA, describe the arc of the circle GAJ. With C as centre and distance CB, describe the similar arc KBH. At the points E and F (where these circles intersect), as centre, describe the arcs JK and GH.

ground by two stakes and divide it into three equal parts. With the length of one of those parts as the radius, and with the two inner stakes as centres, trace two circles which will cut each other at two points equal distance from the main axis and which will mark the shorter axis on the figure. Place a stake at each of these points, and from each one of these as a centre, and with twice the radius formerly used, describe the arc of a circle which will connect with the circumferences of the smaller circles. The outline of the figure is now complete.

A rougher method and one much more generally used, is to first mark the major axis. At a distance slightly less than one third of that axis, and from one end of it, drive another stake. From the other end of the line measure off the same distance and drive another stake. Now take a cord fastened loosely to each of

With AB as the major axis, insert stakes at D and C. Fasten a cord to the two stakes D and C, but long enough to pass round B. Removing B, and keeping the cord drawn tight, mark the outline of the figure, as atbBi.

the inner stakes and of such a length that it will just slip over one of the end stakes, then removing this end stake to use as a marker and holding the line perfectly tight, move around the foci, firmly marking the outline of the figure desired.

THE MAKING OF CURVES

As a matter of fact precision in tracing curves for outlines of borders along the lawn is not necessary. This is true even when carrying out an exactly drawn plan on paper. It must always be borne in mind that these curves are not to be taken in a bird's eye view. They will not be looked at from above but from the front. Therefore after the general scheme has been staked out on the ground the final positions should not be accepted without considerable experiment in varying the position of the stakes to see that the most happy arrangement has been made. Long sweeping curves can generally be marked by eye better than by any mechanical means. The director of the work should stand at some fixed point and have an assistant carrying a supply of pointed stakes which he places in the ground as instructed. By shifting them backward and forward, and from side to side, most pleasing effects can easily be produced.

In very few cases are regular curves really necessary. Occasionally, however, as in making turns for carriage drives, it is desirable that true results be obtained. In tracing contra curves it is very desirable that they be very nearly true, and especially if these are parallel as might be the case in extending a turf walk from the lawn proper to the other parts of the garden. In these cases one curve should be traced first by the eye and, the stakes having been finally driven, the opposite curve is then laid by a reproduction of the first.

We will suppose a straight line. The garden line may be used to mark this. The two ends of the line should mark the extreme ends of the contra curve which will cross the line exactly at its centre. Measuring from the beginning of one curve to the point of intersection between the curve and garden line, find the centre, and from that measure the distance to the outline of the curve. Lay it off similarly on the opposite side of the line to mark the other half of the contra curve. From the point of intersection with the perpendicular and the original curve draw a line to the starting point, and another to the point where the curve intersects the straight line. From these bases measurements may be taken as necessary for reproduction of the other half of the curve. This is the simplest form of laying a curve but the method can be adapted to more complicated figures by merely increasing the number of base lines. The essential point to be guarded, and the one which it is most easy to trip over, is in making the curve continuous where it changes direction at the point of crossing the guide or straight line.

OBSTACLES AND CURVES

Every change of curve made in a walk or a border or a driveway should have, must have indeed, its real or apparent reason. Merely winding walks are a nuisance and tiresome. They will not even be used. A "short cut" will inevitably be made, resulting in a complete cutting up of the lawn into irregularly formed patches. A curve, though of itself beautiful, becomes irksome when laid on the ground without any support or reason. At the same time straight lines should generally be avoided. Therefore masses of shrubbery, a flower bed, an old tree retained from the original clearing, or a rock abutting from the ground, should be worked into the scheme. These "obstacles" may not be merely natural features. They can be imported or artificially made. The number and variety of the curves must be in proportion to the surface and contour of the ground. The more hilly or undulating it is the more numerous may be the curves. The entrance from the public road is made at right angles so as to give the greatest ease of approach from all directions. But if there is room the curve should begin immediately inside the ground, a reason for its doing so being established by a judicious planting or flower bed.

A convenient width for a walk is eight feet, with half that width for side paths over which there is not traffic.

PLANTING GROUPS OF TREES In planting small isolated groups of trees or shrubs the triangle should form the basis in every case. The equilateral triangle, however, should be avoided, as should the very commonly seen method of planting five trees in a rough circular form with a sixth in the centre. A far better effect would be obtained by planting only five, for instance, in a four-sided figure, no two sides of which were of the same length the odd specimen being placed in the centre. Before planting, stakes should be driven in and moved about until a satisfactory composition is reached. Neither should the group be regarded from one point of view only. Naturally there will be one main aspect for every group, and sometimes it will be so compelling as to preclude the possibility of adjustment from other points of view. The situation will then be met by secondary or subsidiary groupings of low growing shrubs in the desired direction. When groups or masses consist of more than half a dozen specimens they should be considered, structurally, as consisting of several groups, and the individual plants should be regarded as forming points of various triangles.

Why a poor soil is preferred Special grasses Worms and their "casts" Watering, rolling, feeding and other care.

A PUTTING GREEN differs fundamentally from a lawn; the only association of the two lies in the fact that both consist of grass. The golfer demands a green upon which the ball may be played with the same delicacy and precision of touch as the billiard player seeks in the bed of his table. But there is this difference; while the billiard table must be an absolute level, the putting green must have a rolling or undulating surface.

As to the grass: what is needed is a short, very dense, springy turf on a very firm soil-bed. The grass therefore must be of a very fine-leaved kind, which will make a growth so close to the ground as to be almost a part of it. For these reasons it is evident that the Kentucky blue grass (or any other of the poas) is quite unsuitable. On the other 150

Two radically different styles of treatment. In the upper view there is open treatment planted for perspective effect, with the lawn itself as the chief subject: all the lines converge in the distance. In the lower picture the lawn is merely the groundwork on which plants and garden furniture are displayed

LAWN PICTURES II hand the bents and the fescues without clover answer admirably.

As to the soil preparation: here again the requirements are quite distinct from those indicated for an ornamental lawn. To help the fine, short growth, a poor, sandy seed bed and an abundantly drained sub-soil (preferably of gravel) is necessary. For a lawn make the soil rich anu deep; for a putting green make it shallow, and dry. If the course lies on a clay or loam, import sand sea sand if possible. Seeding should be much thicker than for lawns say twice the quantities recommended earlier.

Mr. Walter J. Travis, the well known world's golf champion, writes thus:

"How many players appreciate how important a part putting plays in the game of golf? In a general way, every one realises the value of good putting. A good putt covers a multitude of shortcomings through the green.

"Considering, then, how very important a feature in the game putting really is it becomes highly desirable that the greens should be the subject of the most intelligent care and attention. Putting is, practically, the heart and soul the quintessence of golf.

It calls for judgment, confidence, coolness, and delicacy of touch.

"I have played over a number of greens on 'the other side," and, while I admit that they enjoy greater climatic advantages, which go far toward making their greens naturally better than ours, yet I cannot recall a single course which possesses better putting greens than we have at present at Garden City; and few approach them in excellence, so far as trueness and turf are concerned.

"They are in such excellent shape, principally by reason of the methods adopted in their up-building and maintenance; owing, also, a great deal, to the natural advantages in the way of a coarse sand-and-gravel foundation.

"It is quite within the reach of most courses to closely approximate such greens even where the soil conditions are vastly different if proper attention is given the subject, hand in hand with unremitting care. Let me briefly outline the general conditions governing the proper treatment of a green.

SPRING WORK

"In the early spring, immediately after the frost is out of the ground, a man should go carefully over such parts as are not entirely covered with grass, with a nail tamper procurable at any of the leading seedsmen's followed by another man, who carefully scatters grass seed into the holes made. At the same time a thin coating of carefully screened, rich loam should be sprinkled over the surface treated. By indenting the ground with innumerable small holes you are sure of getting the seed to stay just where it is wanted, instead of its being blown away by the wind or washed away by the first rainfall, especially if it is on a slope.

"Work of this kind can also be done at any time from April until October; but, in the summer months, it must be followed up by continuous watering until the grass is fairly well started. If for any reason the new grass fails to materialise, keep at the work until it does. It is impossible to have too close a carpet of grass on a green. Where nine-tenths of the ground is covered, the balance being made up of bare spots here and there, it is very easy to get the whole covered. These bare spots are usually caused by rolling down worm casts. Before a green is cut or rolled, the green should be brushed. The better, and in the end the most economical plan, is to get rid of the offending worms by applying a mixture of corrosive sublimate see page 157-

FEEDING

"Do not put fertilisers of any kind on a green except, perhaps, some bone dust, and then only once every three or four years. If the soil is very poor a thin top dressing of well-screened loam, plentifully mixed with seed, may be applied in the spring. The chief trouble with most greens, however, is that the soil is too rich and the grass is, consequently, coarse.

"Probably, the best seed mixture for greens is Rhode Island bent and creeping bent in equal proportions. These thrive well in nearly all kinds of soil. A coarse green can be very sensibly improved by seeding with this mixture every season, and also by the use of sand in the late fall and early spring.

"Whenever a weed of any kind shows itself it should at once be cut out and a pinch of seed put in. In the early years of a green, before the grass is well established, weeds will appear, and the only thing to do is to systematically go over the entire green every season and cut them out with a sharp knife as far down at the roots as possible. And the same way with crab or summer grass. This treatment, faithfully pursued for a season or two, followed by careful seeding, will make it almost impossible for weeds to find a lodgment.

WATERING

"During the hot and dry summer months the greens should be thoroughly soaked at least twice a week by letting the water run through a revolving sprinkler. If necessary keep the water going all day, moving the sprinklers from time to time. Watering in this way, even under a hot sun, is infinitely better than just wetting the surface in the evening. The latter practice, in point of fact, does more harm than good, as it results in the roots of the grass bunching themselves close to the surface the only place where the moisture is instead of boring down, as they should. Therefore don't be afraid to soak a green. No injurious effects will come from the hot sun pouring down its rays if watering is done during the daytime. On the contrary much good is done as the water is usually cold sometimes very cold and the sun offsets this, which is not the case when the water is applied at night.

MOWING AND ROLLING

"Cutting a green seems a simple thing, but it is well to remember that no green should be cut twice with the mower running the same way. If it was cut north and south last time, run the mowers east and west next time, and so on, alternately. If cut circularly, reverse in the same way. Not only does this insure a much cleaner, trimmer, cut, but it improves the grass.

"Except in the early spring, just after the frost is out of the ground, a heavy roller should not be used on a green. Even then it is better not to do so unless the ground has been badly worked up by the frost. The use of a heavy roller tends to make the grass root-bound and materially injures any green. All greens should be rolled at least once a week with a comparatively light roller the ordinary garden roller. Those with three sections are the best. Finally, a roller should be pulled never pushed. If pushed, and the ground be soft, the footprints of the man are left; and, anyway, a man digs in his toes more when pushing than in pulling.

"Another thing: do not, under any circumstances, keep players off the regular greens at any time. The more they are played on, the better, irrespective of time or weather conditions. Play on them day in and day out, the year around. They will be improved by it, although it is hard to believe this when the frost is coming out of the ground, and deep heel-marks are left by the players. Rolling will correct this.

GETTING RID OF WORMS

"Worms once in seem to flourish and multiply if left to themselves. Thousands were got rid of in one year by sprinkling soap-suds on the infested patches, but great care had to be taken on account of the presence of alkali in the mixture. In 1902 I tried a solution of corrosive sublimate (bichloride of mercury). The formula is I to 256 i., one part of corrosive sublimate to 256 parts of water. Three to four pints of this solution mixed with a barrelful of water forty to fifty gallons answers tiie purpose admirably and without the slightest fear of injury to the grass. Undiluted it is a very active poison and requires careful handling. "The most economical way of applying it to the greens is to erect a scaffolding five or six feet high at the highest point alongside the green or an empty wagon will do and place thereon a couple of empty kerosene barrels, with a hole bored in the bottom, into which run a piece of three-quarter inch hose, sufficient in length to cover the entire green. Connect the hose with an ordinary sprinkling can and sprinkle freely. That's all. It is better to have a couple of barrels so that one can be filling while the other is in use. When filled pour in the mixture and stir. The barrel being elevated the water will flow by gravitation with sufficient force to keep the sprinkler going until the contents of the barrel are exhausted. There is just enough poison in the mixture to put an absolute quietus on every worm that's touched. After they come to the surface they never go back again, and can easily be brushed up at the end of the operation. The grass is not injuriously effected in the slightest degree, nor are cattle or sheep that may be allowed to graze on it.

"The best times to treat greens are early in spring or in the fall, when the ground is soft and the worms are 'working." They are then nearer the surface and 'rise' much more readily than when the ground is harder, when more of the mixture is required.

"If a green is treated in the spring comparatively few worms will be in evidence in the fall. But if any are left it is better economy to get rid of them. Unless their 'casts' are removed before the green is cut or rolled it means the final ruination of the green. The labour and consequent expense involved in first brushing off the 'casts' represents a big item, and it is better economy to get rid of the pest at the outset."

It may be added that since Mr. Travis wrote the above, trials of other grasses have been made, with the result that the fine-leaved fescue is being used now in conjunction with the bents. The crested dogs-tail, which makes a very low turf, with very firm leaves, and stands hard usage, will often be found a good grass for a putting-green, and may be used as indicated on page 104.

A tabular presentation of the essential differences of the seventeen standard lawn grasses, their soil preferences, and uses; prices, weights, and quantities to sow.

lour as Kentuc mixes well wi d bottom gra mended alone.

Same and A g ery rapid grow r able for short quck Is practically an ann uplands r, sha s.

seful in mixture for the Northwes and for lands o poorest sands.

pes on lawns n dry, high tions.

effects on the Mideastern

CPSIA information can be obtained at www.ICGtesting.com
Printed in the USA
BVOW02s1957091213

338615BV00003B/516/P